Small Space
Big Living

Small Space

Interior design to make every inch count

Big Living

SOFIE HEPWORTH

FRANCES
LINCOLN

Contents

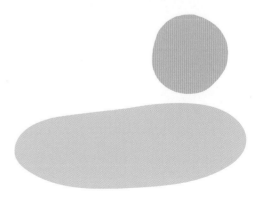

Introduction

As I write these words, my family and I have been living in a 40sqm (450sqft) studio house for a poetic 365 days. And hand on heart, in those 365 days I have learned more about interior design and what truly makes for a happy home than in my entire 38 years prior!

For those of you who don't already know me through my Instagram account and website, *Three Boys and a Pink Bath*, my name's Sofie and I'm a serial renovator, a self-confessed interiors addict and a colour lover! Ever since I held the keys to my first house – a basement flat in Blackheath in London – I have been obsessed with designing and creating a beautiful home.

I have long been fascinated with small-space design. I've spent hours watching *Tiny House Nation* and *George Clarke's Amazing Spaces*. There's something mesmerizing about seeing a family of four comfortably sleeping in a decked-out campervan! I guess it's the level of creativity and ingenuity required to make a modest space successful – it gets me super excited. And back in April 2020, I got the unique opportunity to create my very own ...

After outgrowing our Edwardian semi in East London, my husband and I set our sights on a rather tired Victorian coach house with few redeeming features in Tunbridge Wells, Kent. I love a challenge; I'm drawn to the romantic idea that every ugly duckling can be turned into a beautiful (and highly functional) swan. Give me the worst house on the street, the project everyone else is too afraid to take on, or the pesky box-boiler room that can't possibly become useful – I'll take them all! But there was one challenge we really weren't expecting. You guessed it! We completed on our new house just one week before the Covid-19 pandemic hit the UK and we were thrown into total lockdown. But rather than crying into my dusty renovation, which would be unlikely to be started, let alone finished, in the next few years, I spotted an opportunity.

Introducing the Sheila Shed!

Sheila Shed is a 40sqm (450sqft) studio that we built at the bottom of our new garden. The decision to build a small home to house our family of four through what we knew would be a long and challenging renovation project was actually a pretty easy one. Given that our home would not be habitable during the renovation process, the alternatives were renting an additional property off site – a lot of wasted money coming straight out of our renovation budget! – or purchasing a caravan, which after significant research and consideration, we decided would quite possibly have finished us all off … and so, the Sheila Shed concept was born.

We took some of the budget out of our larger renovation pot and put it towards creating a tiny home, which we knew would add value to our property in the long run. After the renovation, we will be transforming it into an incredible guest house for our friends and family, a dedicated workspace and, possibly, an Airbnb rental further down the line. Even longer term, it could become a teenage boy's dream hangout (read: escape from the parents!).

I have been posting on social media about my renovation projects for some time now, but this one seemed to strike a chord. Since the start of our journey, Sheila Shed has featured in a plethora of leading interior-design magazines and digital and print media, including on the front cover of the *Sunday Times Home* supplement. It's been praised by the world's leading interior-design community, and hailed as a triumph in small-space design, and as a showcase in the future of small-space, multipurpose living. It's been a total dream come true – if not a little overwhelming – and has ultimately led me to this point – writing my very first interior-design book.

I want to share all that I discovered during the challenging process of designing, building and living in our tiny house. There is so much to be learned by studying small-space design, and massive benefits to be gained in applying its principles across the board. And although this book is geared towards small-space design, the 'rules' that you will find between these pages can be applied to homes both large and small – whether a humble studio, a classic Victorian terraced house or newbuild family home.

The world of interior design can feel a little exclusive. As an avid consumer of interior-design books and magazines, I have often felt that the spaces on show seem unattainable for everyday people with everyday spaces and everyday budgets. I want to do the opposite with this book: create a stylish, practical and approachable guide (coincidentally, my goal in interior design, too!) that shows you, through simple, easy-to-follow dos and don'ts that you too can create a home that looks professionally designed, no matter the size of your space or your budget.

This book is unpretentious, honest and real — just like me. I'm not an interior designer to the stars; I'm not someone who has had the luxury of employing professionals to help me, or someone who has always been able to buy the best that money can buy. Sheila Shed was a self-build project; designed, built and decorated by my husband and me, with only a small amount of help from specialist tradespeople. I hope this will give you the confidence to believe that you too can achieve magazine-worthy interiors without professional help.

Using Sheila Shed as our guide — and everything she taught me along the way — I'm going to walk you through the process of creating a small space with huge impact. I just know we're going to have a lot of fun, so strap in, our small-space design journey starts here.

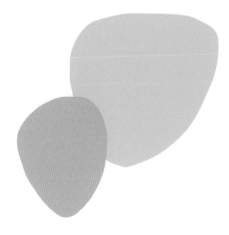

1

SMALL BEGINNINGS

If you have picked up this book, chances are you're feeling a little overwhelmed by the lack of square footage in your life.

Perhaps you're questioning whether it's humanly possible to make your modest studio, crammed terrace or tiny box bedroom look like the impossibly gorgeous and outrageously functional small-space beauties you've been pouring over on Pinterest?

Believe me when I tell you that the answer is YES! Absolutely yes. Size has nothing to do with style. With careful planning, and this trusty book in hand, your small-space project really can be truly spectacular. I promise!

Planning your small-space project

Whether you're tackling an entire self-build, a top-to-toe renovation, attempting to squeeze a home office in without a dedicated room, or simply looking to update one challenging room in your home, this book contains advice to help make your project a huge success.

Whatever the space you're working with, every project starts in the same way: with a detailed plan. I cannot stress enough the importance of planning when it comes to interior design, especially if you're not blessed with generous space. The first step in a new direction is always the most daunting, so in this chapter I'm going to walk you through some of the 'must-dos' at the early planning stage. Get these down and you'll soon be running towards your design goal!

The list of everything ever

The very first thing you need to do when designing your small space is write what I like to refer to as 'The List'. Professional architects and interior designers call this a 'Design Brief'.

Obvious though it may seem, the most common mistake I see friends and family making when designing their homes is rushing into the fun parts of the project. Buying 'that table' before the space has even been built because they simply love it; ordering some cushions they saw on an Instagram post last week because they looked 'oh so fabulous' in that influencer's home; or hastily picking a paint colour based on the latest trending shade at Farrow & Ball.

Sound like you?! I applaud your enthusiasm, I really do, but please – step away from the credit card! There is much for us to do before the shopping can begin, and never is this more important than when designing small. So, what is The List and how will it help you?

Those who have the luxury of an architect or professional interior designer will be asked to complete a detailed design brief, which includes their ultimate wish list. It is likely to include a series of questions, such as:

'What is the function of this space?'
'What items does the space need to store?'
'How should the space look and feel?'

This wish list will ultimately become the designer's bible and will influence every decision they make for their clients for the duration of a project.

No budget for a professional? Don't worry, I've got you. This is a simple task that you can absolutely do on your own, and it will be the single most important step in your design journey. Throughout the process, I encourage you to continually refer back to The List; however, The List should also be flexible enough to allow for changes as your project develops, and to account for any unexpected curve balls thrown your way (don't stress, curve balls are a part of every design project).

Why does this space need to be created?	We need a multifunctional tiny house to live in while we renovate our uninhabitable home. The space needs to function short term as a family home for four people, and long term as a guesthouse, home office and possible Airbnb.
Who will live in or use the space?	Sofie aged 38. Rob aged 40. Teddy aged 7. Reggie aged 5
What will they use the space for?	Sofie: sleeping, eating, working, relaxing. Rob: sleeping, eating, working, relaxing. Teddy: sleeping, eating, working, playing. Reggie: sleeping, eating, working, playing
How do you want the space to feel?	Contemporary. Comfortable. Like a holiday. Inside-outside. Center Parcs meets Bali meets Ikea tiny house advert.
How do you want the space to look?	Fresh, bright, colourful, fun, unexpected, flawless, unique.
What items must the space or house store?	1 x kitchen (oven, two-burner hob, kettle, sink, crockery) 1 x sofa 2 x single mattresses for kids 1 x king-size bed for two adults 1 x computer Storage for paperwork and stationery Up to x 4 chairs for dining and work 1 x desk that ideally can seat a minimum of two adults 1 x dining table that can seat all four family members Kids' toys, books and games Plants, home accessories and soft furnishings
What are the challenges with the project?	The site is narrow and long, with built-up banks on the site, so limited opportunities for windows. The space has many jobs to do, and this is extremely challenging given the footprint. The budget is stretched and needs to be focused on essential spend first.
Will you use any builders, tradespeople or professionals to help? If so, what for?	We will do as much as possible ourselves to save budget, but we may need to employ: Electrician, Handyman/carpenter
What is the budget for the project?	£65,000 approximately
Is there any contingency?	Possibly an extra £5–10K

The List can be built out as much as you find helpful, but I would recommend using the example on the previous page as your starting point. Taking the time to sit down and really think through your project in this level of detail will ensure that form can meet function without any compromises, which is the ultimate measure of success in a small-space design project.

From this point forward The List should be your reference point for every decision you make. As we gather more information and start to make decisions throughout the process, you will want to update and build out the list further. For example, once we start to allocate parts of the budget to parts of the project, you may need to adjust the items on your wish list accordingly. Which brings us nicely onto our next point …

Budgeting

Where to start? It can be tough to know how much a project is going to cost, especially when material and labour costs are constantly evolving in line with the economy. From my own experience, and that of others I have spoken to, it can be extremely tempting to pluck random numbers out of thin air. It's funny how when we do this, the numbers happen to perfectly align with the money we have allocated to the project. Sound familiar? Thought so. Right, let's do this properly then guys!

You need to be extremely realistic about how much you can afford to spend, and the true costs of the labour and materials required to complete your project. Denial and guesswork are not going to help; both will leave you with either an unattainable brief, or worse, a half-finished project! Remember, there is ALWAYS a compromise, and it's better to control what that compromise is, than to find yourself short on cash, unable to purchase or pay for an essential item, or have your project come to a grinding halt.

When approaching budgets, as with design, I've found it helps to break it down into stages – starting with top level, essential costs and then slowly adding in detail. That way you won't break into a sweat when staring down at the pound signs and abandon your project all together.

The back of an envelope budget

Step 1

Regardless of the size or scale of your project, the first thing you need to do is create a basic 'back of an envelope' budget. This will determine whether a) the project is feasible, and b) whether the budget required is even remotely close to the money you have or can access.

This first basic budget should include all the large, obvious costs for materials, labour and big-ticket items such as fixtures and fittings. This document may start with a bunch of question marks, but with a little time searching online, asking friends and family and gathering quotes, you should have a pretty good idea of what costs to allocate to which trades, materials and purchases. It can also be helpful to include some of your 'must-have' (translation: 'really want') luxury items in this first list, as it will help you understand where your compromises lie and identify areas where expectations or budgets may need to be adjusted. Lastly, when allocating your money, do so on a price range from lowest to highest. By doing this you are building in a contingency and outlining both your best- and worst-case scenarios. It is important to know that if everything costs just a little bit more than you expected that you can still afford it.

If you are planning a self-build or a larger project that requires planning permission and may involve an architect, you are going to need to spend a lot more time on this initial budgeting phase.

Gathering quotes from tradespeople can be very time consuming. They are typically very busy, and quoting for larger projects takes time, so you may need to reach out to a lot more individuals or companies than you want quotes from. Being ghosted by a tradesperson is a normal part of this process, so don't take it personally! If they don't respond, they don't want the job and therefore you won't want to work with them either.

While you are gathering quotes (see page 24 for my tips on finding the right tradespeople), you can still populate your back of an envelope budget with some ballpark figures. There are widely recognized pricing calculations used by developers, architects and designers will give you a price based on the square footage of your space and the type of build. Asking local neighbours, friends and family who have recently completed similar projects is another great way to get a quick and accurate idea of pricing in your area.

The purpose of the back of an envelope budget is to quickly assess if your plans are plausible, and if you have, or can access, the sort of money indicated in this initial budget. There are going to be many more line items added later, so it's important to recognize that this stage is simply to help you decide whether pushing on is worth your time and energy.

Example: Back of an envelope budget for a simple room update

ESSENTIAL HIGH-LEVEL COSTS	
Plastering x 3 days at £300 a day	£900–£1,500
Electrician x 2 days at £500 a day	£1,000–£1,500
Flooring 10sqm (108sqft) at £100 psqm	£1,000
King-size bed from Shop-X	£400
Wardrobes x 2 Ikea	£400
New radiator	£150
LUXURY ITEMS	
Professional decorator x 4 days at £200 per day	£800
New bedding	£100

TOTAL ESSENTIAL BUDGET = £3,850

TOTAL BUDGET INCLUDING LUXURY ITEMS = £4,750

If it looks like your initial vision is way out of reach, go back to The List and try adjusting the size, scope and requirements of your project, then redo your back of the envelope budget until it starts to align with your financial reality. If the total comes back broadly aligned to what you were expecting, and more importantly, what you can afford, move on to Step 2. The detailed budget (see opposite).

Example: Back of an envelope budget for an extensive project with average costs

ESSENTIAL HIGH-LEVEL COSTS

Architect fees	£5,000–£15,000
Planning fees	£1,000–£2,000
Building regulation fees	£1,700
Electric and plumbing	£2,000–£4,500
Foundations/ground works	£2,000–£3,000
Brickwork	£3,000–£5,000
Plastering	£1,500–£3,000
Rendering	£850–£2,700
Roofing	£2,000–£4,000

LUXURY ITEMS

Professional decorator x 6 days at £200 per day	£1,200
Carpenter for bespoke cabinet	£10,000

The detailed budget

Step 2

Once you have assessed the high-level costs, spoken to local tradespeople and gathered quotes, you will need to start budgeting in much more detail. In the early stages, I would advise including as much detail as possible. This will massively decrease the chances of finding yourself in camp 'ran out of money' – no one wants to be in that camp believe me, it sucks.

When budgeting, it's all too easy to overlook smaller items, but overlooking something like 'structural engineering' or not allocating a budget for 'switches and sockets' can easily equate to finding yourself thousands of pounds short and unable to finish. My advice is to overestimate and include absolutely everything on your wish list, however small it may seem. In this way, you are building a worst-case scenario budget. If things start getting tight during the process, you can start to strip items out, switch to cheaper alternatives, move certain tasks to a later date, or move them on to your DIY list.

Your budget document will be something you need to keep a close eye on and regularly update throughout your project. As a guideline, for Sheila Shed I would update both The List and my budgeting document on at least a weekly basis. Checking off your lists, budgets and progress will also help you sleep at night! Renovators' insomnia, caused by the many hundreds of decisions required to finish an interior-design project, is 100 per cent a real thing. From experience, lists and planning are about the only things that ward off unwanted late-night panic attacks.

Your detailed budget should also include a timeline for each of the line items, and a simple cashflow to show when you have money coming in and money going out. A basic cashflow document of this type is going to be crucial if you are tackling a larger, more involved project.

PLANNING & PRE-BUILD COSTS

Planning	£150	I did the planning and design myself as I was confident. I referred to recent planning applications in my local area that had been approved for similar garden self-builds.
Architect	£0	We did not use an architect as again I felt competent designing and building the space without one. Allow a budget of between 3-15% of your build costs depending on the complexity of your project and the support you need.
Site Survey (PTOs)	£150	We had protected trees so we needed to get advice on what we could and couldn't do. Depending on your site you may need to budget for this.
Council Fees	£200	Various fees relating to applications to cut down trees. Budget to cover site visits and a change of driveway application.
Solicitor's Fees	£0	You may need to allocate budget for solicitors if you are building near a boundary.

SITE AND GROUNDWORK COSTS

Site Excavation	£2,800	This sum will vary dramatically depening on your site. We had to move a lot of earth and build a small retaining wall. We did what we could ourselves to save money and then handed over to a contractor to dig out a large section of earth.
Drainage	£900	This sum will vary dramatically site to site. We had to connect our foul in the studio to a main drain. We got very lucky with the location of the drain and it was a simple job. Drainage can run into many thousands if you are not located near a mains-drain.
Ground Screws	£2,160	We used ground screws as our foundations. These are eco-friendly, quick, and cheaper than concrete.
Small Concrete Pad	£1,000	We had to pour a small concrete pad for under the outdoor bath.

BUILDING MATERIAL COSTS

Timber for structure *	£11,000	Hob	£345
Insulation	£1,200	Tap	£120
Cladding	£8,000	Kitchen Sink	£150
Roofing Membrane	£1,500	Lighting	£300
Roof Adhesive	£230	**OUTDOOR AREA**	
WINDOWS & DOORS		Outdoor Bath	£2,000
Roof Light	£1,600	Planting	£1,400
Doors, Front	£1,500	Decking	£2,300
Window	£500	**LABOUR**	
French Doors, back	£1,300	Labour ***	£15,000
UTILITIES		**SOFT FURNISHINGS**	
Electrics	£1,500	Soft Furnishings	£1,400
Plumbing	£2,000	**TOTAL**	£66,304
Hot water cylinder & pipework	£1,600		
KITCHEN			
Kitchenette	£1,500		
Internal Furniture Timber **	£2,000		
Oven	£499		

* Our studio was timber built and this was therefore one of the biggest costs.

** We built all the wood furniture ourselves. This saved us tens of thousands of pounds in carpentry. If you are not DIY inclined you will either need to budget for a carpenter or more off-the-shelf furniture.

*** We did a huge amount of the work ourselves, labour would have been much higher if we hadn't.

Gathering quotes and finding the right tradespeople

If you don't already have a black book bursting with reliable and well-priced tradespeople, this part of the project can be a little nerve wracking. Handing over your hard-earned cash to people you don't know is a big step, and feeling apprehensive about this is perfectly understandable, so here are my top tips for finding the right team for your project.

1. Keep it local – Local, independent building firms and/or tradespeople rely heavily on their reputation and word of mouth referrals within their area. Hiring trades or firms that work in your local vicinity not only means you are more likely to know, or find, someone who has used their services already and can vouch for their work, but also increases the likelihood they are going to work hard to make sure you are satisfied. One bad review in a small community can be devastating for individuals or businesses, so chances are they will work extremely hard to maintain a positive reputation.

2. Go for a walk – Every time I am about to embark on a major building project, I spend an afternoon walking around my local area looking for houses having similar work done. There are often signs up outside properties advertising the firms involved in the works, and if there aren't, simply knocking on the door or asking the builders outside for their details is a great place to start. Seeing the quality of the work being done in the flesh, how tidy the site is, and how the builders behave on the job is all invaluable.

3. Friends and family – Getting the details of a recommended tradesperson recently used by friends, family or acquaintances is the closest to risk free you are going to get. If friends and family haven't come up with suggestions, try extending the message out to school and/or work WhatsApp groups, local Facebook pages, community forums and anywhere else with several local people you can ask. Most people are very happy to recommend their trades professional if they had a great experience and are also more likely to let you come and have a look at the work done – which is gold dust.

4. Builders/review sites – While I personally wouldn't hire someone just off the back of a builders' review site (such as Check A Trade or MyBuilder), these sites can be very valuable when used in conjunction with Steps 1 to 3. They help build a bigger picture of how long the individual or company has been in business, how many jobs they have successfully completed and what their customers say about them.

5. Get social – As a visual person, one of the first things I do when looking to hire a company or buy a large-ticket item for my home, is check social media (usually Instagram). Companies and trades with a social media presence are not hiding from customer reviews and often share images of their work that are real, rather than stock imagery or heavily edited. Trade websites that use stock imagery and do not feature any real-life projects make me very nervous, so I always head to Instagram. It doesn't matter if they don't have a large following or don't get many likes, it can be tricky for small businesses to run their social media accounts and their businesses too, but just having a presence is a great sign that they are confident of good reviews, happy to show off their work and are reliant on their reputation. It's a good indication of a professional person and/or company who is proud of their work and has nothing to hide. Once you have identified a company or trade you want to get quotes from, you need to have a list of questions ready to ask them. Here are mine – I would encourage you to use these and add to them as you see fit.

- How long have you been in business?
- How many years has the business been doing this type of work? (Especially important if you are employing a specialist or niche skill.)
- Can you show me some examples of other similar projects you have completed?
- What insurance do you have?
- Is there a customer locally who would let me come and see your work?
- Can I have references from similar projects you have completed?
- What guarantees does the work have?
- What are your payment terms? (Note: you should NEVER hand over the entire cost of the project upfront).
- How long do you anticipate the project will take?
- How many projects do you take on at once?
- How many staff do you have? And who is responsible for managing them?
- How do you deal with issues, errors or challenges with customers?

Creating a floor plan

So, what is a floor plan and why is it so important? A floor plan is a scaled diagram of a room or building from a bird's-eye view. The floor plan may show the entire building or a single room. Your floor plan should include measurements, furniture, soft furnishings such as rugs, appliances and anything else you have included on The List (you didn't think I'd forgotten The List, did you?).

Before I talk more about floor plans, I want to remind you that I am someone who discovered my love of interiors and talent for design later in life. I do not have any formal interior-design qualifications, and no one has ever taught me how to do this. But why am I telling you this? You are here to learn from a professional, right? I'm doing so to remind you that even someone with no professional design qualifications, and no ability to create complex three-dimensional drawings, can design a home that can grace the covers of the world's leading interior-design magazines, and be deemed successful enough to write a book. If I can do it, then so can you!

Yes of course a professional interior designer will be able to produce an incredible floor plan, and beautiful 3D imagery far beyond what you may be able to create, but don't let that intimidate you. You can 100 per cent design a small space that is massively successful without having any professional interior-design skills.

Neglecting to draw up a floor plan early on in your project is the single biggest mistake you could make with your project, especially when it comes to small-space design. But don't panic, you don't need fancy software or wizard-like computer skills to do this, even a floor plan that is hand drawn on graph paper using colouring pencils and a ruler will more than suffice.

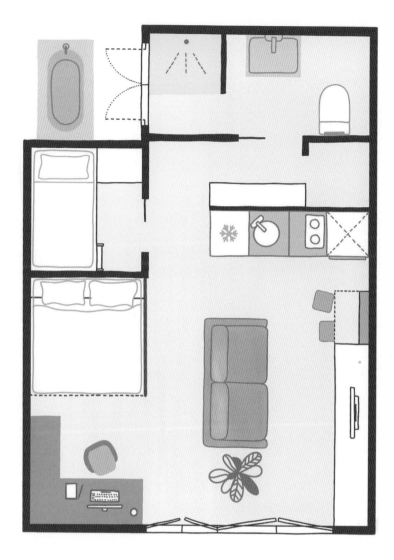

Things to include in your floor plan:
- Precise room/building dimensions
- Location of windows and doors
- Location of power points and light switches if they currently exist
- Furniture placement and sizing
- Zones and walkways
- Views if you have them
- Colour – I like to add colour to my floor plans as it helps me to visualize how the colours will work together in zones

How to draw it

There are heaps of free tools out there for creating floor plans and most are fairly intuitive if you are even just a little computer savvy. However, if you've never done this before – and are perhaps a little intimidated by technology – hand-drawn floor plans are absolutely adequate for the task. I personally tend to produce a heap of hand-drawn floor plans as a starting point, and then use SmartDraw once I am getting closer to what I think the finished floor plan will be. SmartDraw requires little to no technical expertise and has lots of nice features so you can easily add colour, plants, furniture and other details that would be hard to incorporate on a hand-drawn floor plan. There are lots of other similar free tools out there, too.

These three floor plans were alternatives to the one I ultimately moved forward with. My initial hope was to squeeze two-bedroom pods in. Which worked on the floor plan but in real-life compromised the floor space too much!

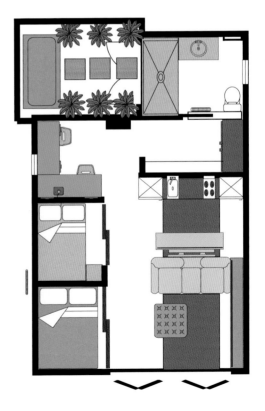

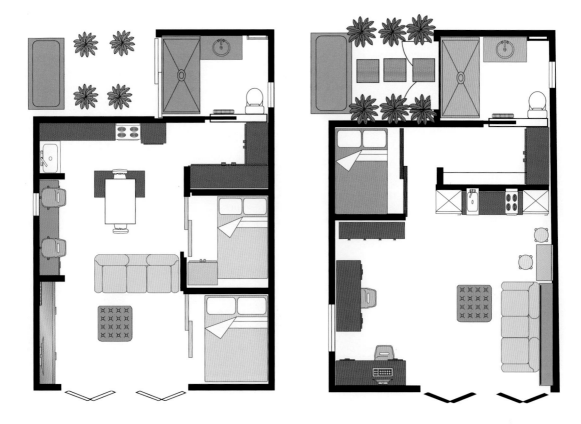

This is precisely what I did with Sheila Shed. I created hundreds of hand-drawn floor plans with my pencil, graph paper and a ruler. I had a few options that I then perfected with SmartDraw. They would all have worked, but it wasn't until the external walls were up and I could see how the space felt that I decided on the layout that I felt would work the best.

What you are trying to establish at this stage is how much space you have, what is going to fit in that space and what the best layout will be, considering any predefined architectural elements, such as doors, windows, access areas, views and plumbing. To get you started, I've provided a step-by-step guide to getting your space down on paper.

Step 1. Measure

The first step in drawing up a floor plan is to get the outline of your space on paper – the size and shape of the room as determined by its exterior walls. To do this, you'll need measurements. Measure your walls from corner to corner using a tape measure. If you have skirting boards, run the tape measure on top of the skirting boards. If there's a lot of furniture or other things in your way, use a stepladder and measure along the ceiling instead.

Step 2. Sketch

Now, take a pencil and a piece of scrap paper and draw a rough sketch of the room. Label each wall with its corresponding measurement. If your space has openings or areas that jut out (such as built-in storage units or alcoves) add those measurements too. Write down metric measurements as a decimal, e.g. 4.5m and the imperial measurements as 10'3¼" (10 feet 3¼ inches). It's worth including both metric and imperial as when you are shopping later down the line you may find that you need both sets of measurements.

Step 3. Draw

Now it's time to draw your floor plan to scale. Grab a pencil (and a rubber!), a ruler and some squared or graph paper. Lay your ruler on your paper and convert your measurements into a scale appropriate for the size of paper and ruler. For example, 5cm on paper might equal 1m in real life, or ½ inch on paper will equal 1 foot in real life. Draw the outline of your room according to your chosen scale.

Step 4. Add windows, walls, doors and built-in furniture

As well as your walls, you'll need to measure doors and any key furniture items, such as your sofa or bed. If the layout is being created for an entirely new area or building, don't forget that you will lose a few centimetres to walls and finishings, and when it comes to small spaces, losing a centimetre here or there can be huge! It's always better to underestimate the finished floor space if it's not yet built and be sure to keep a close eye on your measurements as the walls start going up, adjusting your floor plan to suit.

Draw the walls, windows, doors and any built-in furniture into your floor plan. Draw each window as a set of double lines and each door as a single line with an arc. The single line represents the door, while the arc represents the path it takes when it swings open. Make sure you place each in the right position along the walls in your scale drawing.

There will be unchangeable elements in your space. These could be things like doors and windows, a lower ceiling section, the TV socket, and so on. It's important to capture these accurately as they will impact your entire design.

By way of example, when I start creating the floor plans for Sheila Shed, I had one very important predefined design detail that needed to be worked around. The toilet needed to sit directly above the waste pipe which ran down the length of our garden. This dictated not only the bathroom layout, but also the entire studio layout. If I had not taken this into account early on, I could have ended up spending thousands of extra pounds on connecting waste pipes to the new location, which would have decimated my budget. The layout still works extremely well this way, and you'd never know that we designed the whole space around where the toilet needed to go first!

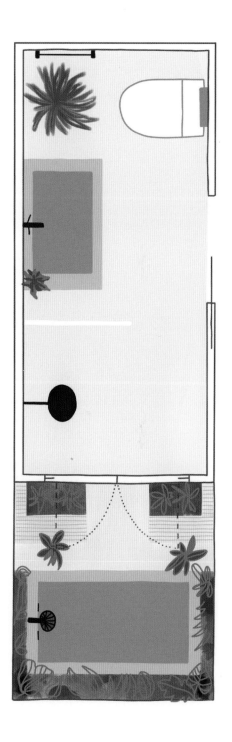

Sheila Shed indoor-outdoor bathroom floorplan. designed around the location of the toilet.

PART ONE: SMALL BEGINNINGS

Step 5. Add your furniture

Adding key furniture pieces to your floorplan is essential. This will help you gain a sense of the flow of the space, the direction of travel around the room or building and ultimately what type of furniture is going to work best in the space. Use your scale to add the furniture into your plan.

If you haven't chosen a particular item yet, looking up the typical dimensions of your largest furniture piece, such as a sofas, beds or tables, is a good start. When designing the Sheila Shed, finding the perfect sized sofa was key to the success of the space, as it was going to need to sit smack bang in the middle of the tiny house. Initially I had penned in a larger sofa, but from experimenting with a two, two-and-a-half- and three-person size sofa on my floor plan, it became clear that a three-person sofa simply wasn't going work in the space. The floor plan told me the sofa dimensions that would allow for enough circulation room in the space; I then used these dimensions to source my sofa.

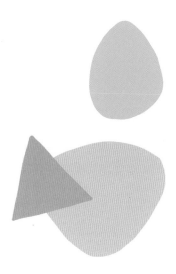

The 3D Floorplan

If you aren't using an interior designer and you don't have the budget to get 3D imagery of your space, you are going to need to find another way to visualize the end product before you commit to any big decisions. For example, where to put your internal walls? Or what size bed can you fit in the space? Sometimes measurements alone are not enough to be confident that the space is going to work.

The quickest and most cost-effective way to do this is to make some simple cardboard models. The goal here is to make a very basic mock-up of your room and any lynchpin items (such as the sofa in Sheila Shed). By doing this you can stand in the space (real or imagined), walk around it, and get a much more accurate feel as to whether your design and furniture selection are going to work. You can then adjust your layout and furniture accordingly.

I know this may sound complicated, but I promise you it's not. If the room doesn't yet exist, tape the floor dimensions out on the floor (if needs be, you can do this outside). This will give you your floorplan in real terms. If your room already exists, then simply stand in the space. Once you are in the room (real or imagined) tape out the size of your key furniture pieces on the floor to show you how far out they sit in the room, then, using cardboard or other building materials you might have laying around (I usually grab boxes from the supermarket, or plasterboard sheets if I have them on-site), build basic pieces of cardboard to the dimensions of your key walls or furniture items.

We are not looking to make a scaled, detailed model here; the focus is on the key measurement that will impact your layout. For example, if you are trying to decide what size sofa you can fit in your space, and the width is your most critical measurement, don't worry too much about making the model the exact same height as your sofa, just focus on the width to see how this sits in the room and whether you have enough space to walk through and around it. Keep adjusting until you are happy with the measurements.

I do this for every single project I work on, big or small. It is the best way to get a clear idea of how the space is going to feel when all the furniture is in it. It's also a great tool to help partners, friends, family and even your builders (who may not have the best vision), to understand the space and what you are trying to achieve.

Locking in your theme

I'm a massive fan of using themes when it comes to interior design. I truly believe that a theme could be the single most useful tool you can use to achieve small-space interior-design perfection!

But here's the thing, the word 'theme' kind of gives me the ick – anyone else? The concept of a themed room instantly conjures images of My Little Pony themed children's bedrooms, or an overly matchy-matchy Barbie-pink themed living room. This is NOT what I want you to think of. I was using the theme method in my interior-design process long before I even realized that was what I was doing. For me, this process is instinctive, and the themes can be so subtle that they might remain completely undetectable to the untrained eye.

Because I tend to theme instinctively, the name or label for my theme often presents itself partway through a project, and not the other way around. But for those less confident, it's going to be useful to decide on a particular theme label early in the design process.

Once you have your theme, you have a brilliant starting point for your search for inspiration, furniture and soft furnishings.

But before we start, let's take a step back and consider what a theme is and define the purpose it serves. The Oxford English Dictionary has the following definition for themes in 'the arts', and I think it perfectly describes how a theme should work in your space.

'an idea that recurs in or pervades a work of art or literature'

In interior design, this recurring idea would present itself in the form of the shapes, colours, materials, textures and the style you select. And when designing small, a theme is going to be extra helpful in defining and unifying the space.

Where to start?

You probably already have some ideas about how you want your space to look or feel, and if not, it can help to reference some widely recognized, broad interior-design themes.

Themes to explore could be:
- Art Deco
- Industrial
- Nautical
- Retro
- Scandinavian
- Boho
- Japandi (a mash-up of Scandinavian simplicity and Japanese minimalism)

But a word of warning here: work with what you have and not against it. Try not to be overly influenced by current fashions or spaces you've seen and loved in other people's homes. Inspiration has incredible value in every design project, but as with fashion, what looks good on someone else won't always look good on you! We are all different sizes, shapes and have different features, and the same is true in our homes. If you are dealing with a low-ceilinged country cottage, you shouldn't be attempting to use a 'Parisian apartment' or an 'industrial warehouse' theme, for example. The architectural features and setting of your space can't be changed, so these should always be your starting point for a theme.

Stand in the space (or space to be), and really study what you see. This might give you some direction on a theme or a mood that feels right.

To give you an example, when I stood in the space where our Sheila Shed indoor-outdoor bathroom now exists, there were no walls or architectural features to observe. It was, however, an extremely secluded, small corner of our garden. It had tall trees hanging over it, birds flying overhead, and it felt serene, magical, wild and very private. This ultimately led me to come up with the theme of a 'Bali spa'. It was this opulent, escapist, otherworldly Bali spa theme that drove every decision I made.

If your space already has some architectural features such as windows, doors, wood, metal/steels or a particular view, e.g., industrial, a cityscape or rolling green fields, your theme needs to work in the context of these.

An Art Deco Mood Board I threw together. Notice the repetition of shapes, colours and textures!

Taking inspiration

Learning (wisely!) from others

So, you've walked into your space and, considering your personal style and the features of your space, you've landed on an art deco theme. What now?

It's time to get collecting! Using the internet, magazines and your camera, put together a range of art deco images that you love (Pinterest is going to be your best friend for this) and write down a list of all the common features of that particular style.

In this theme, features you would observe might include:
- Brass, mirror, chrome and glass lacquer as materials for furnishings and accessories
- Velvets and sensuous animal-skin fabrics, such as shark and zebra skin, for seating and headboards
- Geometric, trapezoidal, zigzag and chevron shapes and patterns
- Soft curves and circles
- Jagged, pointed edges inspired by skyscrapers (such as the Chrysler building in New York)
- Colours are striking and bold, but often paired with high-shine metals or monochrome accents

Learning from other people's success in interior design is incredibly important. Sometimes it can be hard to see why a space is so successful, but you can absolutely recognize that it works, and when it does, we need to try and understand why. This does not mean attempting to make a carbon copy of a space you love – you will never achieve the exact same feeling or look and anyway, you will get so much more satisfaction from creating a space that is uniquely yours. Have the confidence to do you own thing, it will pay dividends in the end.

Making the theme your own

Sofie with an F style...

Because I am not a trained interior designer, my approach
to interiors is largely instinctive. Never is this truer than
in my use of themes.

While broad, widely used interior-design styles and themes like art
deco are well documented in the world of interior design, my personal
preference is to create a more specific and unique theme to drive my
design choices. This theme is for me, and a useful tool, rather than an
attempt to design to a trend. Tailoring a particular theme to your own
space and preferences will ultimately result in its successful application.

The next few pages show a few examples of themes I have used in
my past designs, what drove them and how I adapted to suit the space.
I hope by sharing some of these wide-ranging themes I have used in
the past, you will feel confident enough and inspired to theme your own
space and pin down your design without getting the ick!

Tribal/jungle theme

Kid's Bedroom

Animal-themed kids' rooms are popular and understandably so, but in my opinion, there is a tendency for this theme to feel a little cookie-cutter and often a tad babyish, which can lead to the room being outgrown all too quickly when newborns turn into 'threenagers' and cartoon elephants no longer feel age appropriate. So, I wanted to take the traditional jungle/animal theme and give it some edge and longevity. I started the design with the bold, giant zebra, which I had seen in a magazine, hanging above a fireplace in a lounge. The zebra led me to the tribal aspect of the theme, inspired by the shapes of the stripes and the monochrome colours. I then started to source tribal inspired pieces that would fit with the theme. I wanted to incorporate colour into the space, and with the room having a Victorian fireplace, high ceilings and elegant coving, I thought a feature ceiling and bold fireplace in Farrow & Ball India Yellow paint would be the perfect way to add a sense of fun and a childlike drama to the theme and the space.

Key features

○ African animal features and prints; the oversized zebra draws the eye in and immediately sets the tone

○ Natural materials for the bed, woven baskets and lightweight curtains to let the light in

○ Tribal patterns on the rugs, bedding and artwork

○ Fringe and tassel details on blinds and rugs

○ Deep, earthy yellow colours paired with monochrome as often seen in tribal design

Desert/zoo theme

Kid's Bedroom

This kid's bedroom was in the same house as the tribal/jungle-themed bedroom (see previous page). When it comes to designing whole houses, the key to unifying all your spaces, is having a 'red thread', which is one unifying feature that connects all the spaces in the home. A red thread could be pretty much anything, from having one colour that repeats in every room to having a series of artworks from the same artists on the wall in each space. The red thread concept works in the same way as a capsule wardrobe: you may have different items, they may be in different colours and be suitable for different occasions, but you should be able to mix and match and still feel like all items (or rooms) are part of the same collection, they work both together and separately, in an infinite number of combinations.

In the case of the property that was home to both the desert/zoo theme and tribal/jungle theme, the red thread was plants/biophilic design. Every room in the house featured a heavy use of plants and a theme that was linked to nature and bringing the outdoors in. This red thread creates familiarity as you journey through the house, bringing different themes and spaces together, making them feel part of the same story.

The desert/zoo themed room came after the tribal/jungle themed room and needed to incorporate plants and nature as part of the overall house vibe. These common facts gave me a lot of direction, even prior to starting the design process: feature ceilings were repeated throughout the house. In this slightly smaller kid's bedroom I started the design with a nature-themed feature ceiling and used cactus wallpaper as the starting point for the design. Feature ceilings like this work well in small spaces that have good ceiling height. Using wallpaper or colour on the walls would have closed the modest space in but using colour or paper on the ceiling adds personality, colour and 'wow', while keeping the walls white and bright maximizes the feeling of space.

Once the cactus wallpaper was in place the desert/zoo theme came naturally and I focused on adding colours, features and details typically associated with nature in the desert.

Key features

○ Repetition of cacti and desert plant motifs in wallpaper, cushions and other accessories

○ Prints of animals you would associate with sandy desert spaces – zebras, camels, giraffes

○ Soft, sandy beiges, sunshine yellows, deep oranges and nature-inspired colours that you would expect to see in the desert

○ Abstract sand-like patterns on the rugs, pots and soft furnishings

○ Rough cottons, paper, flax-like cushions, woven basket light fittings and textured rugs

Industrial/boho penthouse theme

Guest Bedroom

This room is a perfect example of working with what you have architecturally to create an appropriate theme. This bedroom is in a loft extension in an urban London setting. The room had views of rooftops and urban life, which naturally lends itself to a penthouse theme. I was aiming to enhance what was already there and create a space that felt at home among London rooftops. Industrial themes can feel cold and masculine, so to soften the industrial elements I chose to add in an unexpected boho aspect, which included plants, sheepskins, boho artwork, tassels on baskets and other boho styling. Remember, there are no rules, and bringing together two themes just requires confidence and commitment to getting it right.

Key features

- Raw, natural, unfinished materials, as seen both in both nature and industrial designs

- Natural, neutral earth tones in the floor, wood and soft furnishings selected

- Heavy use of plants

- Subtle styling, including tassles, moccasins, boho artwork and fur throws, are a nod to the boho element

Date night hotel theme

Master Bedroom

This master bedroom in an Edwardian property had beautiful period features and a naturally opulent and grown up feeling to it. Considering these features, and knowing that this was to be a master bedroom, the concept of a 'Date night hotel' theme revealed itself. I wanted to step into the room and feel like I was transported to an adults-only, boutique hotel – an escape from mundane day-to-day reality, surrounded by romance, opulence and luxury.

Key features

○ Deep, dark, sensual colours for the walls that create a cocoon-like space

○ Brass fixtures and fittings that add a touch of classy opulence

○ Minimal accessories as expected in a hotel bedroom

○ High-end fabrics in velvet and linen

○ Unexpected, high-quality details such as the bold, deep-green bedsheets

○ Luxe finishing touches in the sockets, wired lamps, flowers and artwork

The mood board

At this point, you will have:

The List – you now know what you want your space to be, what it needs to house/store and how you want it to look and feel

A budget – you know how much money you have available to spend and where you need to spend it

A floor plan – you are clear on what space you have to work with, and the space required for your key furniture items

A theme – you have a theme that will help you select the colours, shapes, styles and features of everything you build or buy

The final thing you need to do before you can make a start on the doing and the buying ('FINALLY', I hear you say), is to bring it all together in a mood board. This will be your visual guide throughout the entire design process.

What is a mood board? Mood boards are a visual representation, or collage, of images, materials, colours, textures, texts and/or any other visual items that communicate an idea, concept or mood. Interior designers create mood boards to showcase their vision for a project, giving their clients a clear idea of what the end product will look like. The mood board may include items already decided upon as well as examples of the type of products we should be looking for to achieve the same look.

Creating your own mood board will give you a clear vision of the end goal of the project, and help you keep it on track throughout the transformation process. Your mood board will also be the first place you see multiple ideas, items and decisions coming together. Your mood board – along with all the other planning elements – is going to keep you focused and should prevent you from losing your way, ordering rogue items that don't work, and making any silly mistakes.

The mood board can, and should be, ever evolving. For example, if you have two beds/chairs/tables/paint colours you are trying to decide between, you should update your mood board with each potential option and compare how each version vibes with everything else on the mood board. There will usually be a clear winner – which will be discovered by good-old gut feeling – this is when your mood board is at its most valuable.

Inspiration in unexpected places

My themes and mood boards are often inspired by random objects or images that are completely unrelated to interiors. The example mood board on page 56 started with an image of a lady in a beautiful outfit that I stumbled across on Pinterest. The colours and textures worked so beautifully together that this was the very first item I placed on my blank mood board and was truly the inspiration behind the entire scheme. The colours in the outfit directed the colour scheme, which featured shades of pink, peach, lilac and army green, and the textures of the outfit influenced the textures used in the room: velvet, matte cotton and shiny brass.

Fashion and nature are two of my favourite places to look for inspiration, especially when I am trying to create a unique, interesting and brave colour scheme. Flowers, birds, butterflies and feathers feature some of the most beautiful colour combinations on the planet, and I will let you in on a secret: nature NEVER gets it wrong! So don't just stick to interior mags, inspiration can come from unexpected places.

On the next few pages, you'll find images of some of the digital mood boards that I've created in the past. Hopefully they'll provide you with some inspiration.

How to create a mood board

A mood board can be digital or physical. Personally, I always produce both, as I believe they serve different purposes and are both extremely valuable.

THE DIGITAL MOOD BOARD

A digital mood board, much like a floorplan, can seem a bit overwhelming for the non tech-savvy among us. But I would urge you to try this on Canva before claiming you don't have the skills to produce a digital mood board. Canva is a free and intuitive tool that allows you to knock up simple but effective mood boards using images you find online in a matter of moments. Simply copy your images and paste them into the board; Canva has an amazing 'background remover' tool that will cut out the section of the images you want in seconds. Digital mood boards are also great for comparing different options or looks at just the click of a mouse. When you are struggling to make a decision, your mood board is going to be your best friend.

I created these two variations of the same mood board for my new kitchen space in the big house. I was trying to decide whether to incorporate the olive green or not. I will often do this at the very early mood board stage to help me decide which direction to go in.

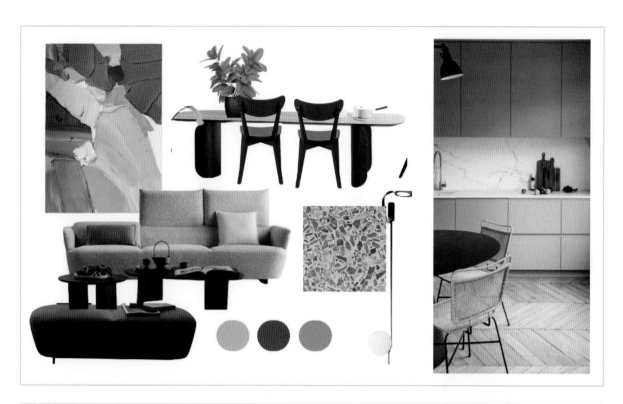

The adult rainbow

This is the mood board I pulled together for a bedroom makeover project I completed in a rental property. My primary inspiration was a picture of a lady in a fabulous outfit that I stumbled across on Pinterest (see Inspiration in unexpected places, page 53). It was the colours used in the outfit that inspired the scheme. Don't be afraid to include non-home/interiors items on your mood board. If an image has the vibe you want to capture in your space, copy and paste it. This super simple mood board started with the colours I wanted, followed by the furniture items. Note the commonality in the shape and form of the pieces I have added – they all feature playful, soft curves and soft edges.

Hopefully you can see that the result very closely mirrors the original mood board in its feel and visual impact. Without the mood board as my visual guide, I wouldn't have been as confident in selecting such unusual colour combinations and bold pieces. This was the most experimental I had ever been with colour, and only by using the mood board as a visual tool to guide me – and seeing the bold colours working so well on that lovely lady on Pinterest – did I execute this adult rainbow bedroom as successfully as I did.

The indoor-outdoor bathroom

This is the mood board I created almost two years prior to completing my Bali spa-inspired indoor-outdoor bathroom. Again, this was a very simple mood board created in Canva using nothing but copy and paste, the background remover tool and lots of inspirational images.

Kid's rainbow room

I produced this mood board for a photoshoot where we needed to create several different nursery looks, at pace, by changing out just a few key pieces. Layering colours, items and furniture as you might expect to see them in the space is not only going to help you nail the execution of your dream space, but it will also inform the all-important 'styling' of the space. For example, I would decide which picture to hang on the left based on this mood board, as well as the order of the cushions!

Hopefully I have now convinced you of the need for, immeasurable power of, and relative ease in creating, a digital mood board. But we haven't quite finished... there's just one more act in our planning phase before we can get cracking with the doing bit! Hoorah!

The physical mood board

While a digital mood board has incredible value, as we have just
seen, nothing quite beats having real-life objects, textures
and colours in your hands.

If you've ever painted a wall and uttered the words, 'but that looks
nothing like it did on their website?!', you will know the importance of
trying things out in your space. Weather conditions, time of day and
professional photography and editing can completely change the colour
of paints and fabrics online, so you are going to want to order samples –
lots of them – and test them together in the exact spot you will be using
them to see if they still work.

Your physical mood board can include just about anything that helps
you define the direction of your project. It might include:

- Colour swatch cards
- Pieces of coloured paper
- Photographs
- Fabric samples
- Illustrations
- Floor samples
- Metal samples
- Printed inspiration images
- Descriptive words
- Colour palettes
- Small items that capture the essence of the space

This is an art, not an exact science, and there really are no rules, so just
have some fun. Ultimately you are aiming to get to a point where your
digital and physical mood boards both look cohesive, you feel like you
have nailed the 'vibe' and your theme and you are confident enough in
your decisions to start ordering.

TOP TIPS

Whenever I am working on a project, I carry around as much of my physical mood board as I can, in my handbag or laptop bag. Then, should I pop into a tile/furniture/paint shop or department store, I can pull out the swatches, fabrics and samples and lay them out next to anything I am considering purchasing. I regularly see people in stores choosing key furniture items like a bed or sofa without any kind of reference to other items in their space or home. It's a big mistake! Go prepared and keep on referring to your mood board. Below is a list of questions you should be asking yourself when selecting items:

- ☐ Does it work with everything else I have?
- ☐ Does it tick off items on my list?
- ☐ Can I afford it?
- ☐ Does it fit on my floor plan?
- ☐ Is it on theme?
- ☐ If I add it to my mood board, does it vibe?

If the answer is yes, to ALL of these questions, then buy, buy, buy, baby!

THE RULES

Small spaces come in many different shapes and sizes and the layout of your space will be the primary driver of your design. Maybe you're working with a long, narrow space with little light; perhaps it's a corner space or a box room. Whichever it is, it's unlikely you've got much flexibility, so it's important that you work with what you have. To help you get started I've picked out some common, small-space layouts and challenges that might look like your own. I've organized them by room and included some tricks and trips that will help you make the most of each space.

The illusion of space

Let's work some magic! Up until this point, my advice and the steps we have completed have not been tailored specifically to small-space design. This is because the planning part of any interior-design project, large or small, should start in the exact same way. But now that our planning is complete (yippee!), and we have a really clear vision of what we want our space to be, and how it should look and feel, I can start to offer up design advice specifically for smaller everyday spaces.

The most powerful and transformative interior-design trick you can use in small spaces is optical illusion. Yup, you heard me right! And no, I'm not talking about sorcery and magic here, gang. There are many easy design tricks we can use that fool the human mind into seeing a space as larger than it is. These are hacks I have spent many years perfecting, so you're in luck.

~~~

Keep the floor clear

You are going to want to keep whatever floor space you have as clear as is humanly possible. Naturally, you'll need furniture in the space you are designing, and this will inevitably cover some of your floor space. But fear not, you can more than make up for that.

Below I have listed some essential small-space adaptations that will increase both the actual and perceived amount of floor space you have:

1. Opt for wall-mounted lights over floor or table lamps.

2. In small-space bathrooms, always go for wall-hung basins and toilets.

3. Mount your TV on the wall (and get those wires chased in or hidden).

4. Where furniture is concerned, opt for lighter looking, less bulky. pieces with slim legs, so that you can see the floor going under the furniture.

5. Where furniture needs to go on the floor, you should aim for it to have multifunctionality and/or adaptability. For example, the ottoman in Sheila shed has storage and contains the kids' trainset and Lego and our kitchen table can be adapted and extended from a two- to a four-person table. This minimizes the number of pieces of furniture required to sit on your floorspace.

6. For furniture fitted to the wall, such as wardrobes, media units, and book and toy storage, opt for shallow but taller pieces. The height maximizes your storage (more about height and the benefits of building up later, see page 76) and the shallow depth keeps your floor space clear, ensuring the furniture won't dominate the room.

7. In office areas go for floating desks and shelves wherever possible.

HERE COMES THE SCIENCE

So why, apart from the widely understood benefits of keeping a tidy home, is keeping the floor space clear so important in small-space design? This is when we get into a spot of science and start to learn about the relationship between what our eyes see, and what our mind believes to be true.

The human mind is a powerful tool. For example, when we read, our eyes scan the words, and our minds fill in the gaps within sentences far quicker than our eyes can process them. The same is true in interior design. When you enter a space, your eyes instinctively scan and absorb the room, quickly assessing the space and sending signals to your brain about what is in place. But our eyes don't look at everything; they scan and transmit information based upon focal points, our brains fill in the gaps and form an estimation of the size of a room based on what our eyes have scanned.

But how can we take advantage of this? By keeping the floor clear, your eyes can journey to the outer most corners of the room, and by opening up the entire floorplan, we perceive the room to be significantly larger than if the exact same space was filled with bulky and deep furniture that projected out into the room. By keeping your floor clear, you will not only be tricked into seeing and thinking there is more space, you will also physically have more space – it's a win, win!

Don't forget your doors!

In most homes I see, the biggest missed design opportunity is in the door selection. I think it's because doors are often inherited, left until last, or even completely forgotten about in the design process.

The contribution of a well-selected door to the success of rooms both large and small should not be underestimated. I always allocate a healthy portion of my budget to good doors, as their power is immeasurable. In small-space design, they are even more important. There are two types of doors that will literally transform a small space: these are pocket doors and glazed doors

THE POWER OF POCKET DOORS

A pocket door is a sliding door that slides into the wall The name 'pocket' describes how, when the door is fully open, it is enclosed within a pocket in the wall — instead of opening outwards the door slides into the pocket in the wall cavity and is completely hidden from view.

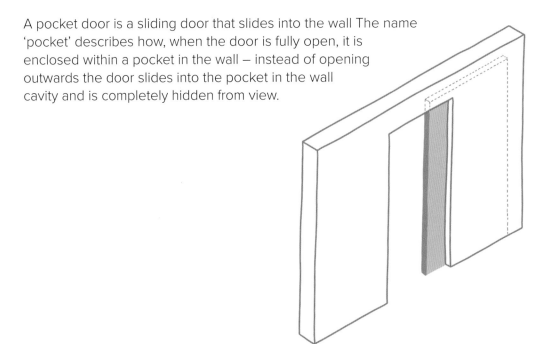

Pocket doors are wizardry when it comes to small-space design (and actually, I use them in my big spaces too). They allow you to use every last centimetre of wall space on either side of the door, ensuring you have no dead space – essential when you are sqft-challenged. They're a little more expensive than your average door, but it's worth it for increased useability; by having a door that doesn't open into a room, the functionality of the space either side of the room is hugely improved.

We used a pocket door between our dressing area and bathroom in Sheila Shed; the space was so compact, a door opening out into either the bathroom or the hallway simply wouldn't have fitted in. By using a pocket door, we were able to use both sides of the wall, maximizing our compact bathroom and our bijou dressing area. And the pocket door is visually more appealing, too – when sliding the door away, you effectively create a view of the next room. It's like framing a piece of art.

Hopefully by now, you are starting to understand that the sense of space is actually just as important, if not more important, than the amount of space you actually have in the success of interior design.

By using pocket doors, you are naturally connecting multiple spaces together, such as the outside and inside, a kitchen and living room or a bedroom and a hallway. They are brilliant contributors to 'flow' in interior design. Flow usually refers to two things:

1. The visual link between the various interior spaces, rooms or zones in a home.

2. The ease with which people can move through a space.

Pocket doors help with flow on both counts. When left open in their pocket, you can see from one space through to the next, creating a link between rooms. Your actual journey through a space is also improved; a swing door can interrupt the flow through repeated opening and closing.

When I'm designing a space, I always think about the views from one room to the next and what you can see in and out of the space if the door is left wide open. It's not always possible, but you should think of your doors as being more like windows, creating a beautiful view through your home.

PART TWO: THE RULES

SLIDING DOORS

Sliding doors open and close along a fixed upper and/or lower track. Whereas a pocket door slides into a wall, a sliding door slides on the outside of the wall. Sliding doors may consist of one door or multiple panels that operate as one unit and slide over one another. In most sliding door configurations, one door remains stationary while the other is movable. The technical term for this type of door is a 'telescopic door', and it was one of these that we used in our teeny-tiny kids' bedroom pod in Sheila Shed.

The kids' bedroom in Sheila Shed is a 2 x 2 metre (6½ x 6½ foot) space and the ONLY reason this pint-sized bedroom works is because of the door selection. By using a glazed, sliding, telescopic door, we have given the illusion of space. One solid wall is effectively removed, allowing you to see into and absorb the space as part of the larger floor plan, while the glass door maintains its function as a separate space.

This choice has also maximized the functionality of the room internally, allowing us to incorporate a large wardrobe, which there wouldn't have been space for if we had used a traditional door that opened into the space. By using glazed doors and a curtain for light control, we are also displaying more of the studio and the connection between the zones and spaces during the day. The glazed doors allow maximum light into this small cubby hole, increasing the sense of space and also showing off the cute design details and colours.

Where you have inherited traditional swing doors, sliding doors have the advantage over pocket doors because they are easier to retro-fit.

Build up, not out

We often forget about the value of vertical space in our homes – by this I mean your ceilings and the uppermost sections of your walls. Off-the-shelf furniture typically maxes out at 2m (6ft), as designers, manufacturers and retailers are looking to maximize the number of homes their furniture can fit into. It's no wonder then that we tend to forget about the space above our heads. While this space may not be as accessible, often requiring steps or ladders to reach it, we should not forget it's value, and particularly not in small spaces.

By building up and not out, you are killing two interior-design birds with one small-space stone. You are creating more floor space (which as we discussed earlier, leads the eye to the outer edges of the room), and by introducing a view high up in the space, you are leading the eye all the way to the ceiling too – somewhere we don't instinctively look. If you have a limited ceiling height, this trick is going to have even more impact. Choose, build or adapt your furniture so that it fills the full height of your space, touching the ceiling. In tandem, you should place furniture at the outermost edges of your room; this will maximize floor space while at the same time drawing the eye to the limits of the room in terms of height, width and depth.

The shelves in the image opposite were purposely fixed to the ceiling; they house books and display items that don't need to be accessed daily. By positioning them on the uppermost part of the wall, we are naturally leading the eye upwards. Once our eyes arrive on the high shelving, they absorb the beautiful colours, display items and design features on this level and enhance the illusion of space. And by keeping the lower wall sections clear of clutter and design details, the room feels spacious to walk into.

TRICK 4

~

Mirrors and reflective materials

I think even novice home decorators will have heard about the power of mirrors when it comes to interior design. But does it really work? Is it actually a thing?

It sure is. Mirrors and other reflective materials are magic when it comes to making even the smallest of spaces seem larger. But why? And more to the point, how? It's a simple concept – mirrors reflect almost 100 per cent of the light that hits them. The more light is reflected into a room, the larger the space feels and looks. In addition, seeing a space reflected back at you tricks your mind into seeing the space in double: the power of optical illusion at its most successful.

To optimize the power of reflective materials and mirrors, you need to be strategic in their placement. If your space has a window, place the mirror on the wall opposite. This will reflect huge amounts of light back into the room, and in reflecting the window provides yet another 'opening' in the room. Whether you are using a mirror in a bathroom, dressing area or simply for decoration, consider using it as a focal point in your design. Position furniture in such a way that the space in front of the mirror is clear and available to soak up and reflect as much light as possible. Hang prints or place objects opposite so that the mirror reflects your design choices and makes your space feel fuller, too.

PART TWO: THE RULES

Goldilocks sizing

When it comes to small spaces, it would make sense to assume that furniture and other items should also be small, right? But this is when it starts to get tricky and a little harder to explain how to get the balance just right. A lot of tiny furniture in a tiny space may in fact make the room look tiny too. So, just call me the Goldilocks of small-space design – not too big, not too small!

The key to getting this right is to focus on the right dimensions, and to select just one or two hero items that are going to feel (notice my choice of word here) full-sized. These hero items are there to grab your attention when you walk into the space, and the attention-grabbing items are where you can play with scale.

In Sheila Shed, the bold, 2.5-person yellow sofa and the full-size, attention-seeking spider light would look equally at home in a room double the size! By designing the space around these two full-size pieces, we are tricking the mind once more. 'Surely a room that can fit a giant light-fitting and a full-size sofa, can't be that small?!' our brain surmises.

But here's the thing. Every other piece of furniture in this space has been purposely adapted to have a slim profile and is on average 20cm (8 inches) shallower than its off-the-shelf equivalent. We are so busy looking at the attention-grabbing sofa and light fitting that we don't even notice the compact nature of the rest of the furniture in the room. We simply assume that everything in the space is of similar scale!

Small-space bathroom

This bathroom is a modest 1.5 x 2.25m (5 x 7.5ft), and yet it looks considerably bigger. This is achieved by combining several of the optical illusion tricks covered in this chapter.

Keeping the floor clear – By selecting a wall-hung basin, toilet and radiator, the entire floor space is kept clear. The eye is led to the far edges of the room, making the space appear considerably larger than it is. If the appliances were fixed to the floor, the space would appear much more cramped. The large format tiles with minimal grout lines add to the illusion of space.

Don't forget your doors! – The pocket doors in this room mean every inch of the bathroom is clear and accessible. They have the added bonus of creating a view from the hallway into the bathroom, and allow the maximum amount of light into the room.

Mirrors and reflective materials – The mirror is positioned opposite the door, helping reflect light from the hallway into the bathroom and vice versa. The glass doors in the shower let light in too and blur the lines between inside and out.

Multifunctionality

Using multifunctional furniture is one of the most powerful small-space design techniques, and a topic that gets me all hot under the collar – it's like Transformers, but for adults! I firmly believe that multifunctional furniture is the future of home design and it's great to see more and more brands embracing this trend, which is driven by the need for our homes to function in a multitude of ways while also maximizing space.

I get a deep sense of satisfaction in finding or designing a piece of furniture that can literally transform itself, your home and your mood in a matter of seconds. No matter the size of your home, an element of multifunctionality and adaptability in your furniture choices should always be considered; it not only boosts functionality, but also allows your home to adapt to your needs as they change throughout the day and night, and over time. But of course, when we are talking pint-sized abodes, multifunctionality is going to wield even greater power.

More than half of the world's population now live in urban areas – and that number is on the rise – so the spaces we live in are shrinking in size. In addition, the way in which we live is fundamentally changing, with the lines between work, home and play becoming increasingly blurred. Our homes are having to work harder than ever before.

The good news is that multifunctional furniture is becoming, not only increasingly popular, but an essential part of furniture design and innovation. With designers and retailers forced to think harder about how to meet emerging interior-design needs, smart, adaptable furniture design is on the rise, with plenty of options to choose from.

From sofas that convert into beds and stools with in-built storage, to folding coffee tables that double as seating, these clever and innovative furniture designs take up less space and serve more than just one purpose, making them ideal for modern-day, multipurpose, small-space living.

If you are designing small, I would urge you to consider incorporating some of my favourite innovative, adaptable furniture pieces into your design. And if you can't find what you are looking for, get creative and make your own, just like we did. See Rule 5: 'Fake it till you make it', page 121, for more information on how to create your own multipurpose furniture.

The multi-use sofa

Sofa beds are one of the earliest examples of multifunctional furniture available to buy on the mass market. This double-duty furniture classic has been a staple in living rooms since the 1980s when futons made their first Western appearance. Thankfully, they've come a long way since hard, uncomfortable and somewhat cumbersome early designs.

Today there are endless options, from beds in a bun, day beds, chair beds and modular sofa beds to pull-out and pull-down sofa beds. All have the advantage of providing comfortable seating in the daytime with the flexibility to transition into a bed as and when needed. And it's not just about sleeping, modular sofas allow you to move sections when needed, too; you can also adapt your seating capacity and living room layout at just a moment's notice.

The storage ottoman

The humble storage ottoman has serious multipurpose prowess. With storage being one of the greatest challenges in small-space design, this double-duty champion should be high up on your wish list. Not only does it serve as a comfortable footrest or stylish coffee table, but its hidden compartment can store a surprising number of blankets, cushions, toys, boardgames, magazines or art supplies – or in the case of Sheila Shed, train track and Lego!

For even more adaptability and flexibility, select an ottoman with wheels – or you can add them yourself. On weekends in the Sheila Shed, we push the sofa (which is on casters) and ottoman to the side of the room – sometimes even outside during summer – allowing the kids heaps of floor space to practise cosmic yoga (their favourite!) or build giant train track networks using the tracks that are neatly tucked away in the ottoman during the week. Flexible living at its best!

Wall-mounted desk

Post-pandemic, working from home has become the new norm for many of us. And for those of us living in small spaces it can feel quite a squeeze. But fear not, for even the smallest of spaces can accommodate a dedicated workspace.

One of the items I've seen making more and more of an appearance in the last couple of years has been the wall-mounted desk, and I LOVE IT. This clever contraption folds up neatly against the wall when not in use, keeping your space clear of clutter (and a clunky desk) for everyday living. When it's time to crack on with your work, simply unfold and voila! You have a functional workstation right at your fingertips.

This type of super compact, wall-mounted desk can be incorporated into just about any space — living room, kitchen-diner, bedroom or even the hallway. Don't work from your kitchen table, it's bad for your back. Find a dedicated slice of wall and make it your very own home office with the help of this simple but super effective, small-space champion.

Nifty nesting tables

We must never underestimate the power of stackable nesting tables, my friends. These beauties are the key to entertaining in small spaces. Nestling snugly on top of one another like a family of interiors Russian dolls, they take up minimal space when not in use. But when the time comes for a soirée, you can whip them out in a jiffy, providing extra surface area for nibbles, coffees or wine.

The marvellous Murphy bed

Ah, the ingenious Murphy bed – a true champion of small-space multitasking. During the day, it is a sleek wall unit, seamlessly blending into your living space. Come nightfall, with a simple pull or fold, it becomes a full-sized bed, providing a restful haven for your slumber.

For those of you not familiar with the term Murphy bed, it is essentially a bed that is hinged at one end or side, allowing for it to be vertically or horizontally folded away inside a cabinet or wardrobe when not in use.

While Murphy beds are having a popularity resurgence due to their highly adaptable, space-saving genius, they still have a way to go when it comes style; there is a tendency for these practical pieces to look a little dated, with a caravan furniture vibe about them. If you are struggling as we did to find an off-the-shelf Murphy bed that works for you aesthetically, consider making your own. The hardware for folding beds is readily available in online stores, and there are plans aplenty on Pinterest, YouTube and Google to help you assemble them. For the more confident among you, a little imagination will help turn this practical piece of furniture into a design statement. Get creative when building the encasement for your hardware (essentially the cupboard that your hardware folds into). Use the opportunity to decorate and enhance your space and add your own signature touch.

If you have an open-plan studio, a multipurpose bedroom-cum-office, or even a lounge in which you want additional sleeping capacity, consider adding a Murphy bed. They come in all standard mattress sizes, so you simply need a wall big enough to house the mattress. Most DIY Murphy bed plans require just timber and the Murphy bed hardware. The process of making your own is akin to making a cupboard, with the hardware itself doing all the tricky engineering for you.

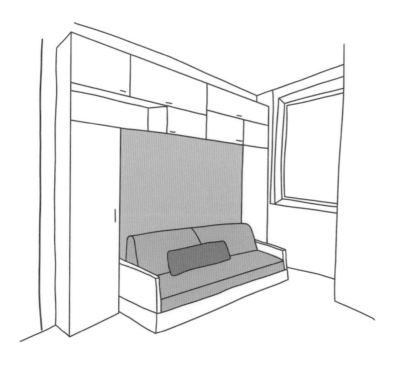

Murphy beds can be horizontal or vertically mounted. In Sheila Shed we went for a vertical Murphy Bed, meaning the bed pulls down from the bottom. If I were creating a multipurpose living room-cum-spare bedroom, I would consider a vertical Murphy bed which converts into a sofa as seen here!

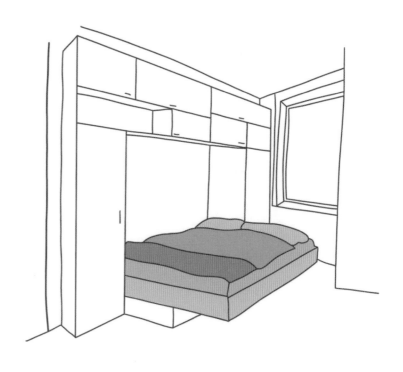

The bookshelf room divider

The bookshelf room divider is a true gem for small-space and open-plan living; it's as powerful in large spaces as it is in the smallest of spaces. Plus, it ticks multiple small space design boxes: creating zones, offering up space to style and injecting personality through your choice of books, plants and ornaments. Like some of the techniques in Rule 1, this item can also contribute to the illusion of space, letting light in from different areas of the house and drawing the eye to the furthest reaches of the room.

Consider using open shelving to separate bedrooms from living areas, living areas from kitchens and kitchens from dining areas. There are plenty of bookshelf room dividers available for varying budgets, from Ikea bargains through to budget-busting, high-end beauties. But when tackling small-space design, I would urge you to consider creating your own shelves; that way they can be made to fit your space down to the last centimetre. This is a simple task for a carpenter, handyman or confident DIY-er.

Ingenious extending tables

When it comes to dinner parties or entertaining guests, tiny-house hosting can be a tall order. Enter the ingenious extending table! A two-person table by day becomes a six-person table by night, magically extending to accommodate more diners. You can enjoy intimate meals with your loved ones on weekdays and seamlessly transform your table into a grand dining setup for guests or on special occasions.

A versatile dining table is likely to be a must have if you are living small or open plan, but the key to it working is ensuring the rest of your space can accommodate the table at its largest. Think carefully about your dining table in relation to the other large furniture items in your home before purchasing, and remember to measure, measure, measure!

May your spaces be small but mighty, and your furniture choices both clever and enchanting. The only thing holding you back now is the limit of your imagination!

Taste the rainbow

Those of you who bought this book because you follow me on Instagram will already know that colour is my passion, and for those of you who bought this book without knowing who I am (firstly, thank you!), I'm guessing you may now have worked this out?!

BUT... and this is important. Just because I love colour and tend to design spaces that are bold and bright doesn't mean that (a) I can only help you design spaces that look just like mine and (b) I don't appreciate or understand other styles and techniques in interior design. I love to absorb, appreciate and break down successful interior design projects that are widely different from my own. It's through studying other approaches that we learn the most.

I have a distinct interior style, one that's hard to put a label on. Designers and journalists have suggested that my style is a form of Scandi-maximalism – a combination of clean lines, minimal fuss, minimal 'stuff' and limited patterns (the Scandi bit) with a heavy use of plants and natural elements and unexpectedly bold colour choices (the maximalist bit). But who needs a label anyway? My style has evolved hugely over the last eight years or so – the time in my life where money has been spent less and less on going out and clothes, and more and more on cushions and paint! During these years, I have experimented with many different colours, tones, styles and hues – and experimentation is an important part of the interior design journey. I have also been influenced by many things and in many different directions: by fashion trends; by other people's design choices; and by what I've found online and in magazines. In my first home, my biggest influence was my own fabulous mum, from whom I inherited my love of interiors.

My mum has a fantastic sense of style (which you can see in the picture of her house above), and our mutual obsession with all things home decor, has brought us much shared joy over the years. When my husband and I bought our first family

home, she was the first person I went to for advice. The classic design of her regal Edwardian home pulled together with a contemporary twist is clear in the first rooms I cautiously designed, such as the lounge in that home shown here.

As my confidence in interior design grew, and the many hours spent and rooms designed mounted up, I began to find my own style. It was through experimenting that I discovered my love for colour and a style, and now I can't imagine veering too far away from this. From white on white on white (LOVE), to opulent dark and moody spaces, colour has the power to evoke feelings and emotions in a way nothing else can.

At this point on your small-space design journey, you will have likely gathered lots of colour samples of your own and have a solid idea of the types of colours you would like to include. But approach with caution – in small spaces we need to be especially careful about how we incorporate colours. In this chapter, I will show you how to use colour effectively in small-space design: from the calm and neutral, to the bold and bright. Whatever your personal preference, you can make it work.

Keeping it neutral

When it comes to small spaces, Google, interior design bloggers, architects, designers and, most recently, ChatGPT will tell you to 'keep it neutral'. Now, I'm not saying that's bad advice, there are sound reasons for keeping your small space neutral.

Ultimately, lighter colours reflect more light and this reflected light creates the illusion of space — the walls, ceilings and surfaces seem to stretch and recede. If you're lucky enough to have natural light in your small space, light-coloured walls and furnishings will extend its reach, bouncing it around the room and reducing shadows. This makes the space feel brighter and more open. Light colours also create a sense of continuity and flow; by employing the same or similar hues on walls, ceilings and floors, you create an uninterrupted expanse of colour and eliminate visual interruptions. This seamless continuity tricks the eye into perceiving a large and cohesive space.

Another advantage of neutrals is their versatility. They serve as a perfect canvas for layering textures and accents. Whether white, beige or grey paint tones, neutrals are easy to live with and go with pretty much everything. However, if not well executed, a neutral scheme runs the risk of looking flat, drab and one-dimensional. To ensure your small-space neutral abode doesn't fall foul of this, consider the following:

Texture is your friend! — Texture is incredibly important when it comes to interior design, but especially when you are working with a neutral scheme. Include a variety of textures, in the form of tactile fabrics, woods, stone and metals. Every item in the space is an opportunity to incorporate texture, from your flooring, cushions, blankets, switches, sockets, art and furniture to your tiles, cupboards and splashback. If you are sticking to neutrals, be sure to add layers of varied textures, from smooth and soft to rough or ridged. Variety in texture allows light to bounce off the surfaces, creating highlights and shadows and transforming neutrals from flat to fabulous.

The north—south divide – Before choosing your neutrals (or any colour scheme for that matter), you need to consider the orientation of your room and the resulting natural light conditions. If you have a dark, north-facing room or one that isn't blessed with much natural light, go for warmer tones. If you are lucky enough to have a light-filled, south-facing room, then all the neutrals will work, but consider the cooler neutrals which balance out the sun's naturally warm light.

Going for bold

The reason Sheila Shed caught so much attention in the press and online is because of the bold use of colour – something that is rarely seen in small-space design.

The trick to incorporating bright colours into small spaces is using a neutral canvas – this allows the colour room to breathe, while ensuring it doesn't overwhelm a space. The logic of 'keeping it neutral' still applies; using white paint on your walls will extend the illusion of space, allowing your bold pieces to shine. Colour should be the paintbrush strokes on your blank canvas: add it through your furniture selections, accessories and artwork. Combined, they'll give the impression of a rainbow room when in reality the space is 85 per cent white.

But beware, it's easy to get carried away. Here are a few tips and tricks for injecting colour without going overboard.

BE STRATEGIC

Focus on creating impact in specific areas. Paint a feature wall or choose a statement piece of furniture as the focal point, like the canary yellow sofa we have in Sheila Shed.

THE POWER OF CONTRAST

Pair bold colours with neutrals to create striking contrasts. This not only adds visual interest but also helps balance the intensity of the bold shades. For instance, a vibrant red sofa against a backdrop of white walls makes a powerful statement.

We rented a property for a period and painting walls was not an option! In this scenario adding colour through soft furnishings was the only way to incorporate personality into what was a rather beige and basic space.

PLAY WITH PATTERNS

Bold colours often go hand-in-hand with patterns. Mix and match different patterns, such as geometric shapes, florals or stripes, to create a lively and dynamic aesthetic. Just remember to keep the scale of the patterns in mind, so that they don't overwhelm the space.

GO MONOCHROMATIC

Don't be afraid to go all-in with a monochromatic colour scheme. Pick a bold shade you love and use various tones and shades of that colour throughout the space. This creates a cohesive and visually impactful design.

TONAL FOR THE WIN

If you've fallen in love with a particular colour, try not to get too matchy-matchy. By this I mean spending days upon days sourcing cushions that are the exact same colour as your wall. Monochrome is fine, but who wants an entirely canary yellow room? For me, a matchy-matchy space means the designer lacks confidence. Instead, try incorporating multiple shades of your favourite colour into your space. This adds depth, interest and professionalism.

Use paint cards

You may have a favourite colour, but perhaps going hell for leather isn't your style. Paint cards are fantastic tools for selecting different colours that work together. Created by colour experts using a ton of science, they're laid out in a way that incorporates colours with similar undertones and hues. Although most people don't realise it, they're designed to make it easy for you to pick colours that work together.

If you want to use three shades of a complementary colour, you should choose three that are next to each other in a vertical column – these shades are a match made in heaven. It's important to note that this rule doesn't only apply to paint – you may have a wall painted in one of your chosen shades of pink and incorporate the other three shades into your soft furnishings, artwork and accessories. This process works in the same way for layering neutrals – it doesn't have to be an explosion of colour, adding tones of neutrals will elevate your space too.

If you want to choose multiple colours that work together, for example a pink and a green, then you should select colours from the same horizontal row. These colours have the same undertones so they will pick up hints in one another.

Be sure to take your paint card out with you wherever you go and check any items you are thinking of buying against the card. It will keep you right on track.

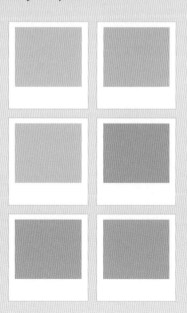

HAVE FUN

Design is an expression of your personality, so don't be afraid to experiment and have fun with colour! Your home should reflect your unique taste and style, so trust your instincts and don't shy away from taking risks.

Colour is a powerful and transformative tool in small-space design. So go ahead, paint the town red, or any other colour that brings you joy!

High definition

Now you know what your colour palette is, and how to apply it, it's time to get painting. But before you pick up that brush, there a few more rules to consider to ensure design success.

Lighting matters
Lighting can greatly affect how colours appear. Test your chosen colours under different lighting conditions to make sure you like them in various conditions. Natural light brings out the truest colours, while warm or cool artificial lighting can drastically alter their appearance.

Sample swatches
Always try before you buy! Paint large patches on the wall in different parts of the space and observe how the colour looks at different times of the day. This will help you to gauge its impact and make any necessary adjustments.

Consider scale
Darker colours can make a small room feel small, so they're best used sparingly. If you love a dark shade, consider using it as an accent or in a larger space within the space to avoid overwhelming the room.

Get in the zone

Right my small-space pals, it's time to talk about one of the most widely referenced yet, in my opinion, underused design tricks in the book – zoning!

Zoning is a simple concept and one you might be familiar with. But for those of you who aren't, let's get right back to basics and start with a simple definition:

'Zoning in interior design refers to the strategic division and organization of a space into distinct functional areas or zones, each designated for a specific purpose or activity. This concept aims to maximize the functionality and efficiency of a space by ensuring that different activities or functions can be carried out harmoniously within the same area.'

(Source: *Residential Interior Design: A Guide to Planning Spaces, Third Edition*, 2016, Maureen Mitton, Courtney Nystuen)

Zoning is particularly essential in open-plan spaces, where multiple activities or functions need to coexist. Sounds straightforward right? Surely, it's just 'cooking zone' in the kitchen, 'sleeping zone' in the bedroom, etc.? Well, no, not exactly. In recent years, the organization of our homes has changed quite dramatically, with a huge rise in the popularity of open-plan living. Alongside the increase in people working from their homes, and the great squeeze (rising prices, smaller properties), zoning has become more important than ever before.

Successful zoning is an art form, and if executed well, has transformative powers both aesthetically and practically. Zoning defines areas by activities, such as living, dining, working, sleeping, playing, entertaining, dressing and bathing. The strategic separation and partitioning of these zones helps to optimize space, enhance functionality and improve overall flow and efficiency. Zoning also contributes to the optical illusion we spoke of earlier in 'The illusion of space' on page 67. A well zoned space will trick our brains into thinking that the space is larger than it is. A correctly zoned room or home is also, fundamentally, pleasing to the eye.

It might sound like stating the obvious in defining each zone in our space but think about a time you've viewed a home either online or in person. There's often that redundant box room or unused corner, incongruous conservatory or lean-to, or an awkward hallway space which has no obvious function. We become instantly wary, primarily because we cannot quickly identify how we would use it or feel about being in the space. By assigning a clear purpose to each area in our home or workplace, we know how to use the space and we can start to picture ourselves going about our lives in it. It is for this reason that home-staging has become essential in maximizing profit in house sales. Even those of us with great vision respond more positively to a well-dressed, zoned and styled space, compared to an empty room, or worse still, a poorly designed one. So much of interior design and a loving home is contained in that illusive 'feeling'. While good interior design won't guarantee you get that 'feeling' it's certainly going to improve the chances of it.

Time to go back to the list. Remember when we talked about the functions your small space needs to enable? Now's the time to start laying them out in zones. I'd hate for you to get to the end of this process and realize your space simply doesn't work on a practical level.

Zone it, baby

So, I think we all understand that zoning is important, if not essential, in small-space design. But how do we do it successfully?

DEFINING THE ZONES

First, you need to identify the distinct purposes of each area of your space. This is going to be easy to do, given that you have your trusty 'List of everything ever' (see page 14) to refer to. Understanding the unique functions of each zone in your space will help guide your design decisions. Once you have your clearly defined zones, and the activities that will take place in each of them, the first thing you need to do is stand in your space and took a good hard look around.

Start by assessing the layout of your space as it currently stands. Look for natural dividers or architectural elements that can assist in separating zones, such as columns, arches, windows, half-walls or natural walkways. Leveraging existing architectural elements will help separate your zones. If your small space lacks any features, fear not, you can create them by clever and strategic zoning strategies – just keep on reading.

PART OF THE FURNITURE

Using furniture to delineate different areas and create boundaries is one of the most simple and effective methods of zoning. By putting our sofa in the middle of the room in Sheila Shed, we created four well-defined zones that made sense both practically and aesthetically.

The sofa is perpendicular to the kitchen area, so acts as a visual barrier almost like a wall, however it doesn't block the flow and allows us to see all the zones working together at once while clearly defining the use of each small space.

ADAPTABLE ZONING

In small-space design, your zones are going to have to work extremely hard to perform the many tasks you need them to. The best way to achieve this is to have zones that can expand and retract as needed, adapting to how you use the space throughout the day and night. We incorporated many adaptable zones in the design of Sheila Shed, without which the space would simply not function for all our many needs.

By installing an extending breakfast-bar-cum-dining-table, we have the option to increase the tiny two-person breakfast bar to a four-person dining table for family dinners. A four-person table would have been far too dominating to remain in place 100 per cent of the time but having the option to extend the dining zone when needed gives the space more usability and flexibility.

Top Table closed – *Breakfast bar style*
Bottom Table open – *Dinner time style*

Adaptable zoning is also important when considering the immediate and longer term use of your space. When we move out of Sheila Shed into the big house, it will become a home office. While one desk is sufficient for the moment, long term we want the option to hold meetings, and invite colleagues, friends and family to work from the space. In addition, we want space for the kids to be able to draw, build Lego and craft. It should be noted that this use was listed as a luxury on my 'tasks the space needed to perform' list, so will have to be extra adaptable to prioritize essential working activities.

With an extending desk, we can have up to three adults working from the space, and/or an adult working and two children playing or doing their homework. This adaptable zoning is at the heart of the success of Sheila Shed and is probably the number one reason we have been able to live comfortably as a family of four in a 40sqm (450sqft) studio.

The foldup chairs neatly hung on the wall is one of my favourite features in Sheila Shed. It's such a simple way to extend the seating capacity when needed and displaying functional things in a beautiful way like this creates a point of interest.

STRUCTURAL ZONING

Zoning isn't always about floorspace, especially in small-space design. There are nifty ways to create entirely new spaces if you're able to alter the structure of your space.

Squeezing a king-size bed into the studio was, without question, the biggest challenge in the design of our pint-sized home. A Murphy bed was the most logical and efficient way to achieve this, however all the Murphy beds I had seen before opened by pulling the door down – this meant our bed would have landed in the open living room, giving us limited privacy and making it difficult for one person to stay up watching TV or relaxing if the other person wanted to go to bed.

So, we took matters into our own hands and designed a DIY Murphy bed where the wall opened out into the room like a door would. This small adaption created a sleep and living zone and a day and night zone, and also offered privacy. Because the wall opens out into the room in this way, it also gave us the opportunity to add the colourful plant pots and greenery to the wall face, which might have otherwise felt purely functional.

COLOUR ZONING

As a colour lover, using colour to define zones is one of my favourite things to do. In Sheila Shed, each zone has its own distinct colour: green for the kitchen, dark yellow for dining, bright yellow for lounging, coral pink for working and rusty red for sleeping. The colours were selected as a scheme and needed to look fantastic both together and apart. This bold use of colour for zoning in a small space works effectively because each brave colour choice is enveloped in a sea of white, creating breathing space around each zone and preventing the colours from either dominating or clashing.

For those who are less colour confident, this technique doesn't have to be so experimental, the idea is simply to use colours to distinguish between the zones, with each zone looking fabulous independently and together as a cohesive scheme.

You can try selecting colours based upon the feelings you want to evoke in each zone. For example, choose warm, earthy tones to create a cozy and inviting atmosphere in your living room. Go for vibrant or cool hues to evoke a fresh and energetic ambiance in your kitchen.

Other simple zoning methods to consider:

Furniture fusion

When it comes to furniture selection, go for pieces that fulfil their functional purpose as detailed in your list, but which also contribute to the overall design scheme. In the living area, consider a compact sofa or lounge chairs that provide comfort without overpowering the space. In the kitchen, opt for sleek, multifunctional furniture that maximizes storage and efficiency. Look for clever solutions like folding dining tables or bar stools that can be tucked away when not in use. Remember, in a small space, every piece counts!

Storage sorcery

Efficient storage solutions are essential for keeping each zone organized and clutter free. Incorporate stylish storage options such as wall-mounted shelves, side tables with hidden compartments, storage ottomans and office drawers with wheels.

Flooring and rugs

Using different flooring materials or rugs to visually separate zones is simple and effective. Hardwood flooring could define your living room, tiles can indicate your kitchen area and a soft rug can define your lounging zone.

Room dividers or screens

Consider using physical dividers like bookshelves, screens or curtains to visually separate areas while still allowing light and airflow.

Lighting

Different lighting fixtures and intensities can highlight specific areas and create visual distinctions between zones. This can be achieved through task lighting, ambient lighting or accent lighting.

• Task Lighting is direct lighting used specifically for certain tasks, such as reading, writing or cooking. Examples of task lighting include under-cabinet lights, guidance lights, table lights and floor lights.

• Ambient lighting is also referred to as general lighting and includes the main lights that you use to illuminate a space. Ambient light also has a way of setting the mood in a room. Examples of ambient lighting include chandeliers, spotlights and track lights.

• Accent Lighting draws attention to particular areas within a space. A wall light positioned above a piece of artwork, or up lights that highlight an architectural feature in your home are examples of accent lighting.

RULE 5

Fake it till you make it

When someone utters the word 'bespoke' in the world of interiors, most of us instantly see pound signs scroll in front of our eyes. It's true that, in some situations, bespoke furniture will cost you more than buying off the shelf. But here's the thing …

When it comes to small-space design, bespoke is pretty much essential for creating a functional and beautiful space. So, after reading through this chapter, I urge you to revisit your budget and consider allocating more to creating furniture and less to purchasing other luxury items. Bespoke furniture could be the difference between good and outstanding when it comes to your small space and I know that bespoke can be cheaper than off the shelf – it just requires a little creativity, the confidence to try and the knowledge you'll be armed with after reading these pages. Let's do this!

Why bespoke?

Bespoke furniture is made specifically for you and your space – for your fireplace niche, your box bedroom, your garden office. Ready-to-buy furniture is designed to appeal to the greatest number of homeowners and to fit into the largest number of spaces possible, to optimize the retailers' potential sales. When dealing with small or awkward spaces, this means you can spend many unfruitful hours desperately searching for an item that not only fits in your space but fits in with your style and theme too. It's enough to drive you crazy, right?

As someone who has spent more time on the internet searching for that 'small-space needle in a haystack' than one would ever consider advisable, I urge you to listen to me right now: STOP. You are never going to find it, and in the time it has taken for you to look, you could have created a unique piece of furniture that not only ticks all your brief requirements and fits the space you are working with but elevates your space in a way off the shelf could never achieve. With bespoke furniture, you are the designer – from the size and shape, to materials, finishes and colours. The only limitation is your imagination. And personally, I just love owning things I know no one else has. Nothing beats that slightly smug, fuzzy feeling when a guest asks: 'Where did you buy that from? It's amazing!' and you casually respond with: 'Oh … we made it'.

The first major benefit of bespoke furniture in small-space design is the efficient use of space. When you have limited square footage, every centimetre counts. Off-the-shelf furniture can often result in awkward gaps or wasted corners, whereas bespoke pieces can accommodate every nook and cranny.

Over the years, I have noticed that many people are nervous about creating bespoke furniture in their homes. I will regularly suggest to friends and family seeking interior advice that the key to their dilemma is, for example, building bespoke bunkbeds with built in wardrobes and toy

storage. But even with tips on how to execute this, they still don't go for it! Admittedly, it's an unusual choice – especially when we are bombarded with adverts for easy-to-assemble, practical and (supposedly) adaptable flat-pack furniture. Perhaps it's a question of cost? Or a lack of creative confidence? Perhaps without seeing a piece first, whether online or in a store, people find it hard to imagine the end product and how it will fit in the space. Well, I'm here to bust some myths. Once you bespoke, you'll never look back.

How to bespoke?

So, you've identified a tricky corner or a particularly tight spot, and you've accepted the fact that a bespoke piece is your only option (exciting!). Now it's time to sketch out a very basic plan of what your piece will look like and measure up the space.

Don't worry, you don't need an art degree to be able to sketch out designs, just grab a pencil and ruler and create a simple line drawing to scale. I find scaled sketches really help me to lock in details like the distance between shelves, the depths of the shelves and the size of cupboard doors. These sketches are also useful for tradespeople.

If you are struggling to nail down what you want to build, this is a great time to seek inspiration from Pinterest. Remember to stick to your theme when searching for ideas, so that the inspiration you receive fits within both your small-space requirements and your style. For example, if your theme is '70s glam' you should be searching for inspiration by using terms like '70s glam bookshelf design'. This will give you an idea of the shapes, materials, style and colours you should be incorporating into your furniture.

Once you have your inspiration, your sketches and your precise measurements, you need to work out how much of your budget is available to produce the bespoke build. In the pages that follow are three different options for going bespoke according to available funds.

A carpenter, the bespoke Rolls-Royce

Option 1

A carpenter will be able to make pretty much anything your heart desires, but using one is going to be the most expensive route to a bespoke piece of furniture – and simply hiring a carpenter does not guarantee a good outcome. To ensure your money is well spent, carefully consider the following:

The right tradesperson

Carpentry can be very expensive, so you need to be absolutely certain that the person or firm you are using is reputable, and that they have previously created furniture akin to what you are asking them for – preferably many times over! See page 18 for tips on finding good people.

A very clear brief that includes measurements, images, sketches and all the essential requirements

Tradespeople, while skilled at what they do, are not usually creatives. Of course, there are exceptions, but I have often seen friends and acquaintances unsure of what they want, asking their builders, plumbers or decorators: 'What do you think I should do?' For the most part, this is a mistake. I have worked with incredible tradespeople with great ideas and plenty of experience; however, tradespeople are not interior designers – they will likely propose practical and commercially focused solutions, with less emphasis on aesthetics. In addition, there is every chance that their taste is very different to yours.

When drawing up your brief, include as much information as possible – the basics such as practical requirements, measurements and materials, but also additional useful pointers such as your initial sketches and images of comparable pieces and other items it will sit alongside.

You must be firm, confident and unwavering in your decisions and your brief. There should be no room for ambiguity on what you are asking for.

Being clear and exact will ensure that the result meets your expectations. And don't be afraid to make absolutely sure your tradesperson completely understands what it is you are asking them to build. In my experience, most tradespeople would much rather work with a customer who has a clear vision of what they want, than one who doesn't, as there is far less chance of an unhappy customer at the end of the process.

Good project management

Keep a very close eye on progress throughout the work and ensure that each stage is going to plan. If you're unsure why something is being done a certain way, then just ask. Don't let this be like that terrible haircut you got where you were too polite to say, 'I hate it, please fix it' and you even tipped the hairdresser before going home and crying into your wine. You are the customer, so it is ok to keep a close eye on the work and ensure that it's going to plan. It's far easier to change something part way through than at the end when it is finished.

~~~

Remember: you should never pay in full, upfront for any trade. If you do, chances are they will be reluctant or refuse to make changes or fix errors once the work is complete.

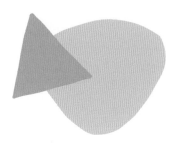

Example: BESPOKE WARDROBE

For fully bespoke carpentry, you're likely to be spending thousands rather than hundreds. But without the specifics of your project, it's impossible for me to say. By way of example, I paid £6,000 for two bespoke wardrobes sprayed in a colour match paint, with all internal wardrobe fittings included.

Since undertaking this project, the cost of timber and labour has gone up substantially and I have seen similar work costing more than £10,000 in the London area. High-end bespoke furniture companies will charge tens of thousands of pounds for built-in-wardrobes, dressing areas and kitchens. Hourly rates for London-based carpenters are usually upwards of £20; however, most carpenters will quote a fixed price for the job which includes their labour, time and materials.

If you're keen to use a carpenter but want to keep costs down, consider compromising on materials. Solid wood is going to come with an extremely hefty price tag – if your intention is to paint the furniture, MDF is going to be far more cost-effective. Even the most expensive off-the-shelf furniture will usually incorporate elements of MDF or similar, cheaper durable materials. If the carpenter's quote comes back a little higher than expected or above budget, don't give up immediately – ask them where you can shave a few pennies. Most carpenters will start by giving a full 'bells and whistles' quote, but there will always be ways to simplify your design and thereby save money.

Is the price worth it? If budget was no question, then personally I would go fully bespoke and enlist a carpenter to build 70 per cent of the furniture in any home, large or small. But given budget is a constraint for us all, we need to make smart decisions on when and where to spend and save.

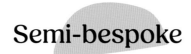

Semi-bespoke

Option 2

If the Rolls-Royce carpentry approach is simply out of reach for you and your budget, fear not, we can get you pretty darn close to a great end result at a fraction of the cost.

Time to revisit our trusty small-space friend, the modular furniture system! Since the dawn of Ikea, modular furniture has opened up infinite possibilities in our homes. Once you understand how to adapt these flexible and highly adaptable pieces to your space, you will be able to transform your furniture from cookie-cutter high-street to high-end bespoke.

So, how does it work? In the case of customization, the modular furniture will form the guts of your piece – by which I mean the insides of your wardrobe, the drawers of your desk or the cubes of your full-height toy-storage unit. It's the doors and frames that cover the modules that become your canvas – paint, cover or embellish to your heart's content. It's the base structure of wardrobes, kitchens and desks that cost the most in terms of carpentry. By buying the skeleton off-the-shelf, you are effectively removing up to 75 per cent of the carpentry work needed and creating a one-of-a-kind piece for much less.

Modular furniture interiors are extremely well designed, often coming in several depth and width measurements, and with adaptable elements – shelves, rails and doors that can be moved to suit your design or adapted over time should your needs change. In addition, these modular interiors are usually made from super practical, hard-wearing and scratch-resistant materials. Something made entirely from wood might look beautiful on day one, but over time will end up scratched and chipped.

Modular furniture interiors are available from so many retailers now. Of course, Ikea is the most well-known, and the 'Ikea hack' is constantly trending for a reason, but be sure to shop around. Most large DIY retailers now have some form of modular furniture system. In Sheila Shed

I used a range from B&Q called Atomia to build almost all the furniture in the space, including our media and toy unit, desk, bookshelves and wardrobes. These cubes and cupboards came in shallow 30cm (12in) depths, perfect for small spaces, and were extremely cost effective, with prices ranging from £25 to £65 per section, depending on size.

Handymen are generally cheaper than carpenters. While they may not work with wood all day long, most will be good all-rounders and capable of making simple shelves, doors and the carpentry to suit this type of job. Handymen will typically charge you by the hour or on a daily rate.

If you are a dab hand at DIY, then you can eliminate the need for a carpenter or handyman altogether! Using modular furniture interiors removes the most skilled elements in furniture making, making it possible for the creatives among us to create pieces quickly and cheaply.

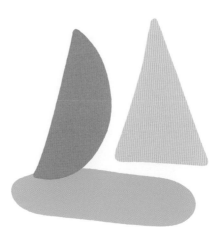

Example: SEMI-BESPOKE TOY STORAGE AND MEDIA UNIT

This media unit attracts so much attention from visitors and on my social channels, and I am frequently asked where we bought it from. I was inspired by a piece of furniture I saw in a magazine in an architect's house that was, no doubt, the real deal.

This piece of furniture was the first we tackled using the B&Q Atomia cube range. We ordered shallow depth cubes with doors and then got a handyman to fit birch plywood to the doors, tops and end panels. This was a fairly simple task for the handyman and the result exceeded my expectations. I love it! If we had built this entirely from birch plywood and used a skilled carpenter, it would have cost more than £4,000 and taken a carpenter a week or more to build from scratch.

COST BREAKDOWN		
Modular top units	£45 x4	£180
Modular bottom units	£45 x4	£180
Birch plywood sheets	£105 x4	£420
Handyman	£100 per day x2	£200
	TOTAL	£980

RULE 6

Let there be light

Welcome to the illuminating world of lighting in small spaces. Where every tiny flicker and every heart-warming glow represents an opportunity to completely transform a space. In petite dwellings, lighting reigns supreme, holding the power to turn dark and dingy cramped quarters into an oasis of welcoming warmth and beauty.

There's no doubt that small spaces present unique challenges when it comes to lighting design, requiring a thoughtful approach to getting the best results in terms of both the functionality and style of the space. In this chapter, we will embark upon on a quest to uncover the secrets of small-space lighting design.

Natural light

In small spaces, the impact of lighting is magnified. It has the power to create an illusion of space, enhance the mood and make the room feel more inviting. The key is to strike a delicate balance between natural and artificial light sources to optimize the functionality and ambiance of the space.

Biological rhythm

Since the dawn of time, humans have evolved around sunshine. Our internal body clocks – what's known as our circadian rhythm, sometimes referred to as the sleep-wake cycle – are finely tuned to the sun's movement across the sky. In simple terms, daylight regulates all bodily functions, impacting our energy levels and the quality of our sleep. The key to a healthy circadian rhythm is the daily reset, triggered by exposure to light and dark.

So powerful is our innate need for light, that should we not be sufficiently exposed to it, we can develop health issues such as seasonal affective disorder (SAD), sometimes referred to as 'winter depression'. Doctors will often prescribe light therapy boxes to address this winter sadness. It is thought that the light (which mimics daylight) causes a chemical change in the brain which lifts the mood and eases the other symptoms of SAD such as feeling tired and/or sleeping too much.

Above *Here the large skylight allows natural light to flood in.*

Using natural light

It's clear how important light is in the context of interior design. As far as possible, we aim to make the most of natural light in our tiny abodes. In addition to using mirrors, glass and reflective materials (see page 79), when looking to enhance the natural light in a space, we should also consider the following:

Light colours – As we discussed earlier, painting your small-space walls in lighter colours will mean they reflect any natural light entering the room, rather than absorbing it, making your space feel larger. In small spaces, be sure to avoid ultra-matte paint, as this also absorbs light; instead, opt for soft sheen which will naturally bounce more light around the room. Note how the white walls and flooring help lighten the space in the picture opposite.

Thoughtful flooring – We don't typically connect our flooring to the light conditions in a room, but we should. In Sheila Shed, the use of a super-white engineered wooden floor, coupled with white walls, dramatically increased the feeling of space and light. Using light-coloured wooden, laminate, tiled or ceramic flooring with a sheen or polished finish will reflect significantly more light than carpets, matte or dark-coloured flooring choices. If you are set on a carpet, consider exchanging it for an area rug, and stick to neutral and light colours.

Furniture – We have talked about the importance of furniture in terms of layout, flow and the functionality of your space, however the selection and positioning of your furniture is just as important when talking about light. Bulkier furniture will absorb light and potentially block some from entering the room. Where possible, avoid putting your largest pieces directly in front of natural light sources such as windows, doors and rooflights.

PART TWO: THE RULES

Artificial light

Before we dive into artificial lighting design techniques, we need to understand the difference and purpose of the two artificial lighting types: architectural lighting and decor-based lighting. Each plays its part in ensuring a space is both well-lit and visually captivating.

When executed well, these two lighting types should work in harmony. By striking the right balance between architectural lighting and decor-based lighting, you can achieve a well-lit and visually captivating small space that fulfils all your functional and aesthetic needs.

ARCHITECTURAL LIGHTING

Architectural lighting is the steward of all things functional, encompassing the practical and foundational aspects of lighting design, illuminating the entire space with even, general light. This type of lighting ensures that every corner of the space can be properly lit. This includes a broad range of lights such as recessed spotlights, track lighting, wall sconces and low-level lighting – the goal is to localize light to exactly where it is needed.

DECOR-BASED LIGHTING

Decor-based lighting, on the other hand, emerges as the hero of style and ambiance. It dazzles us with its ability to set moods, highlight focal points in a room and inject personality into a space. This type of lighting is all about the decorative contribution to a space, and is often selected as a focal point or feature in a room.

The 'Big Light' is rarely switched on and should be chosen not for its illuminating qualities, but to serve as a work of art, enhancing the overall aesthetic appeal of the space. Decor-based lighting is where you can truly let your creativity shine, selecting fixtures that reflect your personal style and contribute to the cohesion of your room's theme and mood.

TOP TIPS

Now that we've met our lighting heroes, it's time for some top tips, specific to the challenge of small-space lighting design.

Embrace the power of natural light: In the battle against darkness, natural light is your greatest ally. Make the most of windows and their positioning in the room. Avoid heavy curtains or blinds that block out the light and opt for sheer or light-filtering window treatments instead. They'll let the sunshine in while still providing a bit of privacy. Strategically place mirrors opposite windows to bounce yet more light into the room.

Champion compact fixtures: In the small spaces, we don't have the luxury of expansive ceilings or sprawling floor plans. That means we need to be creative with our lighting choices. It's all about finding those compact fixtures that pack a punch without overwhelming the space. Sleek wall sconces, slimline pendant lights and recessed lighting will be your best friends. Choose fixtures that have a smaller footprint, allowing you to maximize the use of vertical space and keep things open and airy at the same time.

Master multifunctionality: Small spaces often wear many hats, serving multiple purposes. Your lighting strategy should be adaptable, accommodating the various activities that take place. Seek out adjustable lighting fixtures that can be directed to specific areas as needed, ensuring optimal functionality and versatility. For example, track lighting with adjustable heads could illuminate your work desk during the day and, its focus shifted, light the dining table in the evening.

Illuminate every nook and cranny: No shadow shall escape your gaze! In small spaces, we can't afford to have dark, forgotten corners. Consider using under-cabinet lighting in the kitchen to brighten up those countertops or install wall sconces in tight hallways to create a welcome warmth. Embrace the power of task lighting, my friends. Whether it's a reading nook, a vanity area or a workspace, direct lighting towards these specific zones to make them functional and inviting. By illuminating every corner, you create a sense of balance and harmony throughout the small space.

Employ visual tricks: Once again, visual tricks are our secret weapon. Use lighting placement strategically. For example, direct light towards vertical surfaces such as walls or tall shelves to draw the eye upwards and make the room feel taller. Let pendant lights or chandeliers accentuate high ceilings if you have them and add a touch of grandeur at the same time. The clever use of lighting to enhance architectural features or focal points can create depth and visual interest, making the small space feel larger and more captivating.

Symme-try or not to symmetry

That is the question ...

Humans are naturally drawn to symmetry: we admire the beauty of a simple snowflake, we applaud the team of artistic swimmers creating picture perfect patterns in the water, we gawp in wonder at the Sistine Chapel ceiling. Beauty is a language universally recognized, and more often than not, this is all to do with the power of symmetry.

Symmetry surrounds us, from everyday objects like the humble fork, an office chair, your car or your handbag, and in the natural world a peacock feather, the pattern on a butterfly's wings, or the intricate petals of a rose. Back in the human world, decades of research into sexual attraction and beauty has proven that both men and women find symmetrical faces more appealing. Armed with the knowledge that symmetry and balance contribute significantly to aesthetic appreciation, it's easy to understand why symmetry is going to be so important when designing interiors.

Symmetry in our homes

Symmetry creates visual balance within a space. Balance refers to the distribution of weight in a room, achieved through the arrangement of objects, colours and textures. Achieving balance is crucial because it helps prevent a room from feeling lopsided or chaotic.
So where do we start?

Focal points

Focal points are fundamental to achieving balance in interior design. I'd like you to think about a time you've either designed or walked into a space that was nice, but which seemed to be missing that 'wow' factor. You might like every item in the space – and the room might be beautiful too – but still, something doesn't quite work. This is almost always because there is no focal point. I see it often and I can't stress enough how critical it is to have one. A room with no focal point is like a scone with no jam, my friends – still edible, but undeniably disappointing and a little underwhelming.

In small spaces, a focal point brings even greater purpose and power. The focal point is the first place viewers' eyes land – think of it as the star of the show, around which you should build the rest of your design. In small spaces, focal points not only create an illusion of depth and dimension but distract the eye from the room's size limitations. And, crucially, symmetry builds on this, by creating balance around this focal point and enhancing it even further. So, how do we go about choosing the right focal point?

Start with what's naturally there

Most rooms will have a built-in focal point, be it a beautiful window, a fireplace, a vaulted ceiling, a seascape, a cityscape or an architectural feature such as an arched doorway. The built-in focal point should be the first place your eyes are drawn to when you walk into an empty room. If you are blessed with a built-in focal point, then your job is to design your space around this focal point.

In the case of Sheila Shed, the natural focal point was the rooflight. As this was an entirely new build, we were able to align this with our kitchenette area. When standing in the door into Sheila Shed, your eyes are naturally drawn to the rooflight where the sunlight floods into the space. This sense of harmony is enhanced by the symmetrical layout of the kitchen cupboards behind it. We positioned the spider light in line with the centre of the roof and the kitchenette, further enhancing the skylight as the hero in the space.

Create your own

If you are looking at your space and feel that there's no obvious natural focal point, you'll want to create one. This is not as tricky as it sounds. First, stand in the doorway to your space and think about what focal point might work with your layout, theme and style. It could be an accent or statement wall, a large piece of art, a spectacular light-fitting, a boldly patterned splashback or a striking piece of furniture. The options are endless when it comes to focal points, but the goal is always the same – to create something that pulls the eye, a showstopper around which the rest of the room will be designed.

Focal points for zones

In small spaces, of course, we might not have multiple rooms to play with – rather we'll have multiple zones within a space (see page 109 for more advice on zoning). The trick is to think of each zone in your space as its own tiny room with its very own focal point. Place yourself where the imaginary door to this space would be, or at least the angle at which it will most often be entered and seek out your focal point from there. You'll need to make sure that each focal point doesn't overwhelm or interfere with another. First, ensure you are clearly able to identify your zones and that they are distinct enough spaces with sufficient distance between them; next, make sure each zone has one focal point only – in larger places you can experiment with multiple focal points, but where space is tight, you want to prevent wandering eyes.

In Sheila Shed the focal point for each zone is only visible if you stand in the imaginary doorway to that particular zone, which means there is a natural distance between focal points. You would need to be standing in a different part of the studio to have a visual of the focal point for each particular zone. This removes the potential for clashes. In the pictures opposite you can see the focal point in each zone from its respective 'doorway' in the space.

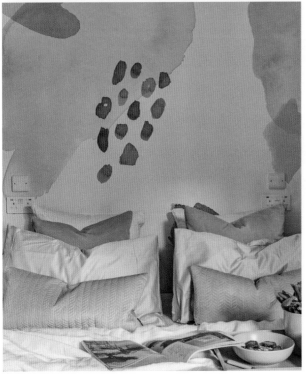

Top The pendant light highlighting the corner in which it hangs can't help but draw the eye. *Bottom left* Without the spots the finish on the wall would look unfocused. *Bottom right* The bold colour of splashback draws attention away from the counter below it.

The devil is in the detail

Once you have established where the focal point is in your space, you can start to add symmetrical design details around it.

Some examples of how to use symmetry and focal points successfully include:

- Using architectural features such fireplaces, doors, windows or kitchen islands that are naturally symmetrical
- Using furniture such as lamps, chairs and mirrors strategically placed on either side of your focal point to create symmetry
- Using art and soft furnishings, such as rugs or cushions, to create identical highlights either side of your focal point
- Using symmetrical wallpaper, or creating a symmetrical colour scheme with paint, that balances both sides of your space
- Adding symmetrical wall lights, or centring feature lights, to further enhance the focal point and symmetry in the room

Identifying and harnessing focal points and then building symmetry around them is one of the most effective ways to achieve balance in your designs. And with balance, comes aesthetic and visual power, as well as feelings of calm and comfort – exactly what we want when designing our small spaces.

Left In this example, the focal point is the fireplace. By placing identical mirrors, lamps and chairs either side of the fireplace, the designer has created harmony, balance and order.

Right In this example, the kitchen island is the focal point. The stools and light fittings frame the sink in the centre beyond it.

Asymmetry

However, rules are there to be broken. You just need to know when and how to break them! Never is this truer than with asymmetry. While symmetry is revered for its ability to create order, there are instances when breaking the rules and embracing asymmetry will yield captivating results. Asymmetry allows for greater flexibility and personal expression.

I speak about avoiding colours schemes that are too 'matchy-matchy' in our discussions on page 104. The same rule applies to symmetry – too much of one thing can be a bad thing. I have seen symmetry become an unhealthy obsession in friends and family less confident in interior design, often to the detriment of the space. This is because symmetry is an easy rule to follow, but a room that is entirely symmetrical shouts 'inexperienced designer'. The thing is, no room is symmetrical in its entirety – there are usually naturally asymmetrical elements to a space, such as the position of the door, a one-sided alcove or an off-centre window. It is our job to work out how to use these natural asymmetries to our advantage and create interest in the space.

Knowing when it's right to go against our symmetrical urges is largely instinctual. Learn to trust your gut and play around – asymmetrical arrangements often reveal themselves through trial and error. For example, you might find yourself rearranging the furniture in a room ten times before finally deciding on the best layout. This is your brain figuring out which layout feels the most cohesive considering the asymmetry of the space and all that's in it.

Symmetry is all about balance, but even with asymmetry, it is crucial to maintain a sense of equilibrium. The key lies in careful consideration of elements such as colour, texture and scale. And don't go overboard – it's about sprinkling in just the right amount so that your focal points remain in place. Like adding a pinch of salt to your favourite dish – you want just enough to make it sing, but not so much that it becomes a salty disaster. Some examples of how to achieve asymmetrical success include:

Off-centre focal points: Instead of placing your focal point dead centre in your space, consider shifting it to one side. For example, position your bold artwork or statement piece of furniture slightly off-centre on a wall. This unexpected placement can add a certain quirkiness and draw attention away from the limited size of the space.
Mix and match: Play with different textures, colours and shapes to create an asymmetrical composition. Think mismatched throw pillows, eclectic furniture arrangements or an assortment of wall shelves in varying sizes. Let your creative juices flow and embrace the beauty of organized chaos.
Dynamic lighting: Use asymmetrical lighting fixtures to add intrigue to your small space. Instead of placing two identical table lamps on your nightstands for example, choose lamps of different heights and styles. Mix and match pendant lights at various heights in the kitchen or dining area. The asymmetry will create visual interest and make your space come alive.

Armed with the power of symmetry and asymmetry, you can transform your small space into a design masterpiece. Experiment and let your imagination run wild. Embrace the symmetrical but don't be afraid of all that is asymmetry – your petite paradise needs them both my friends!

RULE 8

Outside In

I don't know about you, but I went from never having seen or heard of the word 'biophilic' to suddenly not being able flick a page of *Livingetc,* or enjoy my daily Pinterest scroll, without its appearing so often as to result in an irrational shudder. So, what exactly is this seemingly overnight phenomenon and how does it apply to design?

Biophilic design

Word trends are as baffling as food trends (peppered strawberries anyone?), but bafflement aside, biophilic design is an extraordinary weapon in our small-space armoury. So, I will endeavour (as I have throughout this book) to break this design concept down into simple, easy-to-follow steps so that you too can unleash its power.

The Greek word 'biophilia' literally means a love of nature. Like our love of light, us humans have a deeply ingrained desire for regular contact with nature. Biophilic design takes this concept and applies it to the design of our homes and public spaces – in biophilic design we are connecting our built spaces with nature; a process more commonly known as 'bringing the outdoors in'.

Before we look at how to do this, it's important to first understand why we want to do so. More and more of us are living in cities amid the concrete jungles of which they so often comprise, so as much as possible it's important to recreate the tranquillity and rejuvenation of the natural world in our indoor spaces. Studies have shown that exposure to nature, even in small doses, can boost mood, improve concentration and increase productivity. So, if we accept that this is true (which I do and you should), then let us explore how we can blur the lines between inside and out in our homes.

A variety of indoor plants are the way to go when it comes to biophilic design.

Going green

If you've bought this book, chances are that you don't have acres
of space outside your window. You may not even have the luxury
of a balcony but living small doesn't mean you have to miss out on
the benefits of nature. In fact, it's even more important to bring the
outdoors in when you're in a confined environment.

Before we begin, you might notice that some of these tips feature in
other chapters in this book – if you don't understand the importance of
natural light by now then I don't know how to help you! (Just kidding, see
pages 134–143 if you haven't already.) The key is context – in each case,
natural light is being used to serve a different purpose. It is this layering
of design techniques that will elevate your space from the ordinary to the
extraordinary. As we know from our work with multifunctionality (see page
84), anything that can kill two (or more!) birds with one stone is golden
in small-space design.

MAXIMIZE NATURAL LIGHT

This can be achieved by simply opening up your windows to let the
natural light flood in and keeping your window frame treatments minimal
to allow as much sunlight through the opening as possible. Increasing
the degree of natural light not only brightens up your small space but also
connects you to the ever-changing beauty of the outside world. Its power
should never be underestimated.

INDOOR PLANTS

Greenery is going to be your best friend when it comes to biophilic design. Introduce a variety of indoor plants to add life, colour and natural tones to your small space. If floor space is limited, get creative with vertical planters, hanging baskets or wall-mounted planters. Choose plants that thrive indoors and fit your space, such as pothos, spider plants or peace lilies, all of which I opted for in Sheila Shed for ease and maximum impact. Not only do they improve air quality but they also bring a touch of the outdoors inside, blurring the lines between outside and in.

In Sheila Shed, we also installed a built-in planter above the kitchenette. This is a great example of layering design techniques – this simple planter niche contributes to the overall success of the small-space design in multiple ways:

Biophilic design – improving the air quality, bringing the green in.
Enhancing the sense of space – by placing the plants high up we are increasing the sense of space by leading the eye to the highest point of the room. We are also framing the generous ceiling height and preventing the eyes from focusing on the more challenged measurements in the space.
Removing clutter from eyeline – by choosing to have the plants above the eyeline we are keeping the room and sides of our pint-sized kitchenette clear of clutter, further increasing both the illusion of, and the actual, space we have in our kitchen zone.
Zoning – green plants above the green splash back help define the zone of our green kitchenette. The plants also break up what would otherwise have been a large block of white, creating visual interest.

LIVING WALLS

If you want to take your plant game up a gear, consider creating a living wall. Vertical gardens are an innovative way to bring nature indoors, even in the tightest of spaces. Install modular planters or wall-mounted containers and let your green wall become a stunning focal point, packed with lush foliage. Not only will it transform your space into a living, breathing oasis, but it will also act as a natural air purifier.

NATURAL MATERIALS

When it comes to furniture and decor, opt for natural materials that provide a direct connection to the earth. Incorporate elements like wood, bamboo, rattan or cork. These materials not only add an organic touch but also bring texture and visual interest to your space. From a bamboo bookshelf to a wooden coffee table or rattan storage baskets, let nature-inspired materials take centre stage in your small space.

NATURAL COLOUR PALETTE

Choose a colour scheme inspired by nature: earthy tones such as greens, browns and blues are both serene and grounding. Experiment with pops of vibrant colours inspired by flowers or the changing seasons to add a playful touch. Think botanical accent pillows, throws or artwork that brings a sense of the outdoors inside.

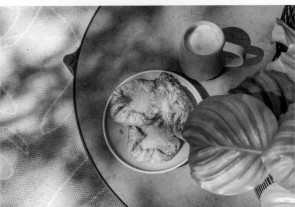

Top The patterm on the throw cushion covers echo the bold leaf shapes of the plants in pots. ***Bottom left*** Soft furnishings in natural earthy colours tone in well. ***Bottom right*** Choose natural materials for an organic touch.

NATURE-INSPIRED ARTWORK

Adorn your walls with artwork that celebrates the beauty of nature. Choose pieces featuring landscapes, botanical illustrations or wildlife photography. These artistic impressions around you will transport you to calming natural settings and evoke a sense of awe. Whether it's a tranquil forest scene or a close-up of blooming flowers, let your walls tell a story of the natural world.

NATURAL TEXTURES

Bring nature's textures indoors to add depth and tactile appeal. Think woven baskets, rattan furniture, cozy wool or jute rugs, and soft linen or cotton fabrics. These natural textures will mimic the feeling of being surrounded by nature. Sink your feet into a plush rug, snuggle up with textured cushions or store your belongings in natural fibre baskets.

MICRO-GARDENING

Even the smallest of spaces can accommodate a micro-garden. Grow herbs, vegetables or flowers in compact containers or hanging pots. Windowsills, balconies and living walls can be transformed into thriving mini gardens. You'll have fresh produce and fragrant blooms, and the deep sense of satisfaction that comes with growing your own plants. Imagine plucking fresh basil leaves or harvesting cherry tomatoes from your own petite garden – a delight for the senses and a visceral connection to the natural cycle of growth.

GREEN VIEWS

Create views of whatever outdoor space you have. Our outdoor bathroom area is a compact 1.75 x 2m (5¾ x 6½ft). It has just two small planting beds in it, which we planted with evergreen ferns. These modestly sized beds and a series of potted bamboo and climbers are so effective that the space (whether you're standing inside or out) feels quite literally like a jungle. You don't need a huge garden to create a home that feels connected with nature, you just need to make greenery a priority when designing your space.

Even though the word gives me shivers, biophilic design is welcome revelation, and it's here to stay. Let these tips inspire you to be creative, playful and resourceful as you weave the outdoors into your daily life. As the American architect Frank Lloyd Wright famously said, 'Study nature, love nature, stay close to nature. It will never fail you.' Or as Sofie with an f, less eloquently, likes to say, 'If in doubt, just add plants!'

If in doubt, just add plants!

RULE 9

Style it out

Congratulations my petite pals, you have made it to the finish line! Styling your space, the icing on the (cup)cake, is the very last step in our small-space-design mini-marathon.

Styling, or home dressing, is the process of making a room look as good as it possibly can while still being functional and expressing your taste. Interior styling comprises many elements in design, some of which we have already discussed in this book, such as:

Optimizing the layout of the room · Implementing clever storage · Adding textures into a room · Using soft furnishings such as curtains, rugs, cushions and throws to dress the space.

In this section, therefore, we'll focus on the finishing touches and home-styling tips that professional interior stylists use to turn great spaces into magazine-front-cover-worthy interiors.

Faffing space

Show off your cool stuff!

Ok, so *Elle Decor* aren't going to call it your faffing space, but this is what I call it and I'd like you to, too. When designing in compact spaces, one of the biggest challenges is the lack of side space. That's the space on our worktops, windows, kitchen islands, sideboards and shelving – these are often the spots that an interior stylist would focus their time and energy on 'dressing'. Using these spaces to showcase your treasures injects personality. Naturally in our tiny temples, we are going to have a limited amount of side space to work with. So, we have to get creative.

Think carefully about which items you think would work best on display and in the context of your theme. Don't cram everything into a tiny corner: open shelves, wall-mounted racks, hooks and floating ledges are your secret weapons here. But don't go overboard: less is more in small space styling – pick a few meaningful items that speak to your soul.

In our previous rental, I added shelves above a radiator. This turned an otherwise dead and nothing kind of space into a destination injected with colour and personality!

Use fewer but impactful pieces

In Sheila Shed, the styling includes colourful artwork, not many decorative objects, minimal clutter on the sides and just a few pieces of standalone furniture. But everything you see has been carefully curated – it's bright, colourful, impactful and contributes to overall design cohesion. With majority white walls and floors, the items we have on display truly stand out. If you are sticking to camp neutral (see page 100) the same rules apply – keep the number of display items to a minimum but make sure they add interest, texture and POW.

The rule of three

The rule of three is well known in the world of design, but for some reason doesn't seem to be common knowledge among the rest of us. When it comes to styling, displaying in odd numbers is rule number one. Whether on a large scale, such as grouping furniture or in a small vignette on a shelf, stick to grouping in odd numbers. Here's why:

Odd numbers have a visually pleasing and harmonious effect on our perception of a space. They create a sense of balance and harmony in a composition. When you have an odd number of elements, the eye is naturally drawn to the centre, creating a focal point. This focal point is visually pleasing and builds a sense of equilibrium in the overall design.

Symmetrical arrangements can sometimes feel too predictable or static. Introducing odd numbers disrupts the symmetry and adds an element of surprise and visual interest. Asymmetry can make a space more dynamic and engaging. If your room feels too symmetrical, then styling in odd numbers and adding in asymmetrical shapes and forms will help to balance the space. You can do this with your cushions, the number of plants on a shelf or the number of photos displayed on a wall.

PART TWO: THE RULES

Height variation

Varying heights of furniture or display items will add depth and dimension. Combining this with the rule of three (or odd numbers) helps to create a sense of hierarchy or priority within a design. The eye is guided through the space and drawn to the most important element, such as your favourite print on your wall. Experiment with heights, you'll soon find a pleasing composition, even if you don't fully understand why it's working.

Texture, layers and tones

As I have demonstrated in my own compact cabana, small spaces don't have to be boring. When it comes to styling, focus on adding texture, layers and tones of colour. Think plump cushions, bold area rugs, blankets slung on sofas. Layering is where the style gods hang, baby! Mix and match different sized pillows and artworks of all shapes and sizes, and throw in some plants for good measure (always). But don't forget to tie everything back to your mood board, colour scheme and theme.

Plants, plants and more plants

Greenery is the easiest way to style. If you're struggling with the finishing touches, just add plants, and give yourself some time to experiment with other items. Plants lift every space they land in. You can also use plants strategically to create the illusion of space. Tall plants like snake plants or ferns will make your room look taller. Don't worry if you're not blessed with a sunny space – there are plenty of low-light plants that thrive in shady spots. Mix and match different types of plants for a lush and lively oasis of texture and botanical shadow.

Showcasing the practical

It's not always going to be possible to store everything away, so instead of fighting it, why not display the practical and make it a feature? In small spaces, it's about finding furniture and storage solutions that pull double duty. We're talking coffee tables with secret compartments or ottomans that moonlight as storage, coffee tables and extra seating (see page 84). And when it comes to decor, choose items that are both beautiful and useful every single time! Wall-mounted hooks are one of my go-tos in small space design – great for keeping your space tidy and a unique way of adding interest to your walls.

Styling small spaces is no easy task, but with faffing space, the rule of three, texture galore, plants-a-plenty and a fusion of form and function, your tiny crib will become a Pinterest-worthy haven. And remember, practise makes perfect, so if doesn't look right first time, keep trying!

THE BONUS ROUND – SMALL-SPACE LAYOUTS

If I had a penny for every time someone asked me to share the floor plans from my interior design projects, I'd be a very wealthy woman! From full house layouts to those for specific spaces like bathrooms, bedrooms and kitchens, accessing successful design ideas can be invaluable for solving small-space challenges. In the final section of this book, we will take a closer look at small-space layouts, addressing some of the most common layout issues encountered in these areas.

Layouts, layouts, layouts

Don't underestimate the importance of getting your room layout right! In my opinion, room layout is the single most crucial factor in the success of any interior design project, whether large or small. A well-functioning space goes beyond aesthetics; after all, what's the use of having a beautiful room if it doesn't serve its purpose?

When designing Sheila Shed, I dedicated about 75 per cent of my time and energy to layout and floorplans. Countless sleepless nights were spent sketching layouts on scraps of paper, followed by endless iterations of the floor plan. It was no small challenge to fit everything a family of four might need into the equivalent of the UK's average-sized one-bedroom flat! The layout of Sheila Shed was always going to be the deciding factor between success and failure.

To save you sleepless nights sketching countless floorplans for a home interior project, consider this book your handy layout cheat sheet. My suggestions, tips and tricks are a culmination of years of measuring, sketches, Pinterest trawling and, finally, designing! I live for a good floor plan, so you don't have to!

Small spaces come in many different shapes and sizes and the layout of your particular space will be the primary driver of your design. Maybe you're working with a long, narrow space with little light; perhaps it's a corner space or a box room. Whichever it is, it's unlikely you've got much flexibility, so it's important that you work with what you have.

To help you get started I've picked out some common, small-space layouts and challenges that might resemble your own. I've organized them by room and included some tricks and trips that will help you make the most of each space.

Small-space kitchens

When it comes to planning small-space kitchens, there are two well-established design approaches that you can use that are aimed at making your space as functional and comfortable as possible. The more traditional approach is the 'kitchen triangle', and the contemporary take on this is to design in 'work zones'. Both are useful concepts to understand when designing small, so let's explore how and why they work.

The kitchen triangle

The kitchen triangle is a design concept that refers to the relative positions of the three main work areas in a kitchen: the sink, the fridge and the cooker or hob. The idea is to use triangles to create a functional and efficient layout, one that makes it easy for the cook to move between these three frequently used areas of the kitchen.

Depending on the size and shape of your kitchen, the triangle will vary. Below and opposite are some examples of the triangle design in a selection of typical compact kitchen layouts.

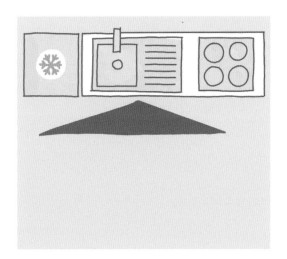

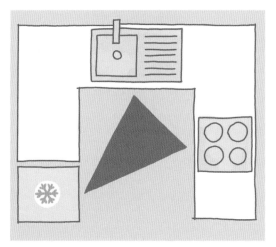

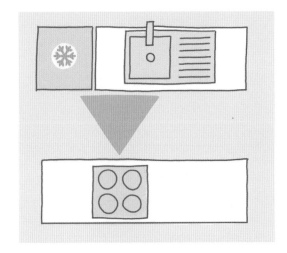

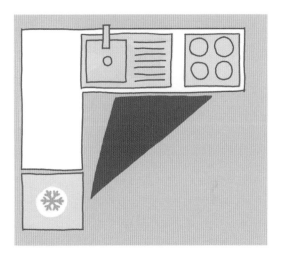

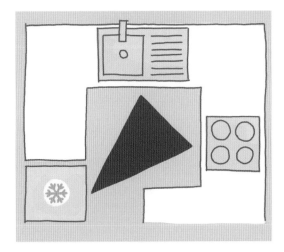

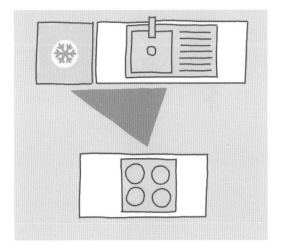

Using the kitchen triangle to guide me, I have created a number of small-space kitchen layouts that will maximize functionality.

The work zone

The increase in the popularity of, and demand for, open-plan, multipurpose kitchens has led kitchen designers to move away from the more rigid working triangle theory, to a work-zone-based approach. This allows for a little more flexibility.

If you have a kitchen with multiple appliances, or one that will be used by multiple people simultaneously for different purposes, then work zones could provide a better use of the space than the triangle. Multiple zones allow two or more people to complete different tasks simultaneously without getting in each other's way.

STEP ONE
IDENTIFY THE FIVE KEY ZONES

Consumables zone: This is the area used to store the majority of your food. You may end up with two consumable zones, one for fresh food (your fridge) and one to house all your dry goods such as food cabinets or pull-out storage.

Non-consumables zone: This is the area used to store non-food items such as crockery, glasses, cutlery, pans and bakeware.

Cooking zone: This is the area that contains your hob, oven and possibly a microwave and/or air fryer, too.

Cleaning zone: If you don't have a separate area for these, this is the area that contains your sink, dishwasher and washing machine.

Preparation zone: This is the area for your kitchen prep. It may be a stretch of countertop, a kitchen island or, as is the case in Sheila Shed, a multipurpose table that doubles as prep space when needed.

STORE RELEVANT ITEMS AS CLOSE AS POSSIBLE TO THEIR RELATED ZONES

CHINA AND CUTLERY
This kitchen zone, used for utensils, cutlery, glasses and small appliances (such a coffee makers and tea kettles), accounts for most 30 per cent of all kitchen storage items.

POTS AND PANS
This area which should be located next to the Food Prep zone contains your large pots, pans, lids and bulk items.

FOOD STORAGE
This area contains both chilled and non-chilled foods and includes both your fridge and freezer.

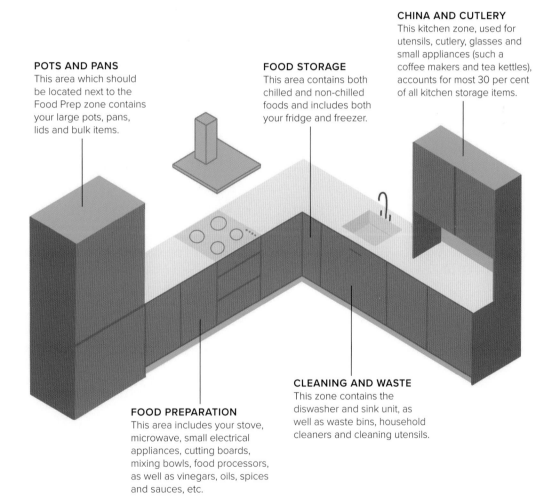

FOOD PREPARATION
This area includes your stove, microwave, small electrical appliances, cutting boards, mixing bowls, food processors, as well as vinegars, oils, spices and sauces, etc.

CLEANING AND WASTE
This zone contains the diswasher and sink unit, as well as waste bins, household cleaners and cleaning utensils.

Work with the space you have

Whether you choose to use the working triangle or a work-zone-based approach will depend on the shape, size and type of your kitchen, plus any personal preferences you may have. If you have a traditional kitchen layout, such as a galley kitchen or U-shaped kitchen, the kitchen triangle can work well. In pocket-sized kitchens like the one seen in Sheila Shed, the triangle can be the easiest way to maximize efficiency.

If you have several options when it comes to layouts, use the list below as a guide to help you choose:

Small, open-plan kitchen/living areas
= single wall

Long, open-plan kitchen/living areas
= peninsular or island

Narrow, separate kitchen = double galley

Square or rectangular kitchen diner
= L-shape

Very small spaces = U-shape; this allows for the greatest number of cupboards in the smallest amount of space

Tips & tricks

INTEGRATE YOUR APPLIANCES

Short on space? Integrate those appliances! Integrated appliances will improve the flow of your space and maximize the storage available (you can squeeze in storage above and below the appliances). In addition, by concealing appliances behind cupboard doors you are further enhancing the illusion of space. More cupboards = bigger kitchen, right?

LET THE LIGHT IN

The more natural light you can get into a small-space kitchen the better. Consider rooflights, glazed doors and glazed sections of walls and windows. White worktop surfaces with a sheen will make the space even brighter by bouncing the light around.

REDUCE CLUTTER

Keep your worktop space as clear as possible for both practical and aesthetic purposes. Consider installing a hot water tap to eliminate the need for a kettle and use deep-drawer storage on lower cabinets so that you can pack away toasters, pans and other larger utensils that you don't need continual access to when not in use.

OPEN SHELVING

Using open shelves in small kitchens is a clever solution. Accessing your crockery and everyday essentials from an open shelf is much more user-friendly than struggling with a clumsy, clattering cupboard door. As well as keeping your kitchen countertop free of clutter, open shelves offer valuable styling opportunities. Choose pieces that are both beautiful and functional to use your shelves to add colour, texture, personality and style. Consider using glass storage jars and colourful crockery, and don't forget to include a plant or two.

CHOOSE COLOURS WISELY

Your small-space kitchen colour scheme should use a limited palette of colours and materials. In Sheila Shed, the predominant use of white accented with a tonal green interior section contributes greatly to maximizing the perceived scale of this pint-sized kitchenette. Colour has been used in a strategic and minimal way to add interest and design flair, without overpowering or closing the space in.

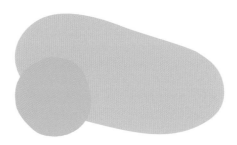

Small-space bathrooms

When it comes to designing a small-space bathroom, the key to success is precise planning. Every element of the design, from your layout, fitting choices, storage solutions and door selection, will be key to ensuring that even the tiniest of bathrooms feels spacious and oozes style.

TOP TIPS

I have created these example small-space bathroom layouts with the following top tips in mind.

- Never put the toilet in-front of the doorway, you want to create a pretty view when you walk in the room. Better to have your sink, bath or shower, opposite the door!
- Consider building half walls to hide toilets, mount sinks or separate showers from other bathroom zones
- Don't be afraid to use the space under windows, it's possible to make a sink work in this area
- Use as much glass and reflective materials as possible

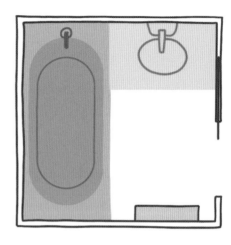

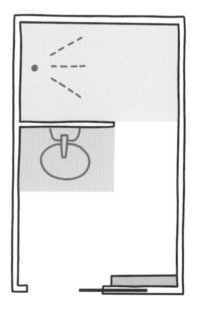

Bathrooms are so personal. Is a shower or bath your Must Have, or does domestic harmony hinge on a basin of your own, or having an entirely separate toilet?

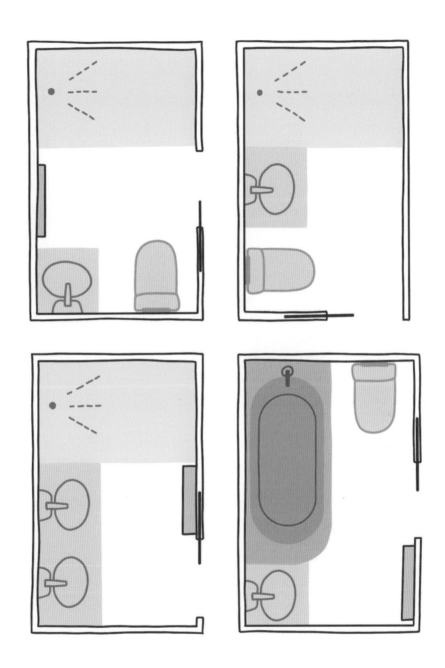

Tips & tricks

CREATE A VIEW!

Focus on creating an attractive view from your doorway into the bathroom. If possible, avoid placing your toilet in front of the door. When you walk into a bathroom you want to be greeted with a view of something beautiful, like a well-dressed basin and mirror, a stunning bathtub or a luxurious shower.

REPLACE TRADITIONAL DOORS

Install pocket doors if you can. This will greatly increase the usable space on both sides of the door. When left open in their pocket, they also frame a view of your beautiful new space. If pocket doors are not an option, consider adding a DIY top-mounted sliding barn door. This can usually be retrofitted where a traditional swing door has been hung. This will give you the same benefits as a pocket door inside your bathroom but does require a little more external space.

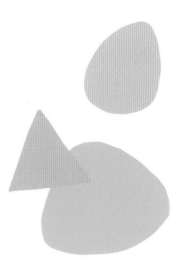

STRATEGICALLY PLACED MIRRORS

If you can, place your mirror opposite a natural light source. This will increase the sense of space and reflect daylight into the room. As well as reflecting light, your mirror should also highlight beautiful features in the room, such as gorgeous tap fittings or the tiling of your new shower unit.

HANG EVERYTHING

Wherever possible, opt for wall-hung basins, toilets and cabinets. They are not only more hygienic and easier to clean, but as we've already seen (see page 82) they also contribute significantly to the illusion of space, showing off every last centimetre of your floorplan.

INCORPORATE GLASS

If your bathroom has an built-in shower in your bath unit, or a shower in a niche, consider a glass side panel rather than a shower curtain, or a half wall of glass instead of a full, solid wall, as I did in the bathroom shown opposite. This dramatically increases the sense of space and light in both the bathroom and inside the shower, while showing off the tiles and fixtures. Placing a mirror opposite the shower increases the light and sense of space, bouncing it and the beautiful views, all around the room.

Small-space hallways

Hallways are the first and last thing we see when we enter a home, so it's vital that we make these first and last impressions count. In addition to packing a punch on the style stakes, hallways also need to work hard functionally to avoid becoming a dumping ground for coats, bags and shoes. However compact your hallway, the key to its success is making it a destination – just because it's not a room you sit in, doesn't mean it shouldn't be treated like one.

PART THREE: SMALL-SPACE LAYOUTS

Tips & tricks

MOVE OR COVER YOUR RADIATORS

In this classic Victorian semi-detached house, the radiator was originally positioned directly in front of the opened door on the opposite side of the hall, meaning the first thing you saw when you walked into the hallway was the radiator! This restricted what could be done aesthetically and made the focal point the radiator (not ideal). Moving it was the first step in making this space work better. By moving the radiator behind the door, we massively improved that first impression.

If moving your radiator isn't an option, covering it is a great second best. Off-the-shelf radiator covers, and/or DIY ones provide you with additional styling space in the form of a shelf — a convenient spot to store keys, wallets and other essentials, or to display stylish trinkets.

USE MIRRORS & GLASS STRATEGICALLY

Glass tables, which dress the space without hiding or covering it, are a good choice as they add to the optical illusion of a generously sized hallway. Mirrors and glass will bounce light around the space, too.

Using glazing to replace a solid wall in a narrow hallway can be truly transformational, drawing light into both spaces and offering an instant wow. Be sure to seek out professional help when undertaking any structural changes.

STATEMENT LIGHT FITTINGS

Don't be afraid to go BIG on your light fitting, however small your hallway or entrance space may be. A striking light fitting will create an instant focal point as you walk into your home.

HIDE THE CLUTTER

Shoes, coats and bags are a hot topic when it comes to entrance halls. If you don't have a dedicated shoe cupboard you are not alone, but the good news is there are tons of options that will hide your deepest darkest hallway secrets, while simultaneously contributing to the overall aesthetic. Look for wall-mounted, slim storage that goes up but not out, maximizing your floor space while providing plenty of storage.

USE COLOUR STRATEGICALLY

While there will be exceptions to this rule, it is usually sensible to keep small halls or entrances neutral. However, colour on front doors, woodwork, light fittings, art and even floor tiles can work extremely well when used in strategically placed small doses. Complementing neutral walls, mirrors and reflective materials with a splash of colour is a great way to make a statement

Get creative and use colour in unexpected places, too. Consider your stair risers, carpet runners, skirting boards and doorframes.

Small-space bedrooms

Bijou bedroom anyone? Fear not, there are plenty of design techniques that will not only maximize space but also ensure your bedroom packs a punch in the style stakes.

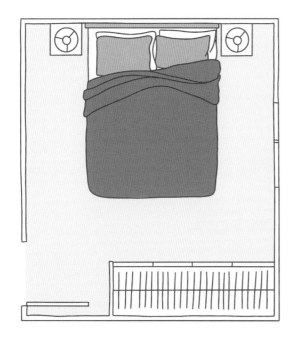

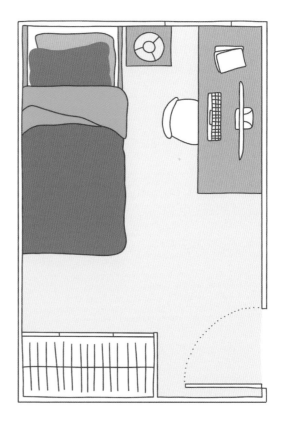

PART THREE: THE BONUS ROUND – SMALL-SPACE LAYOUTS

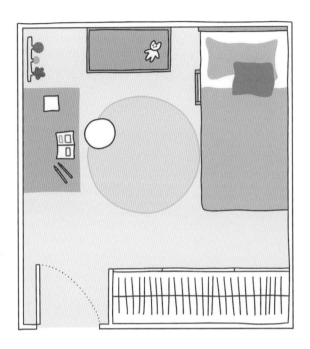

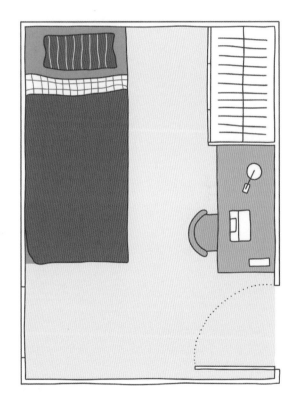

These show configurations for a simple double bed or a single bed incorporating a workspace, homework area or play desk.

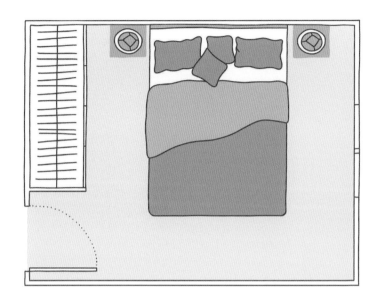

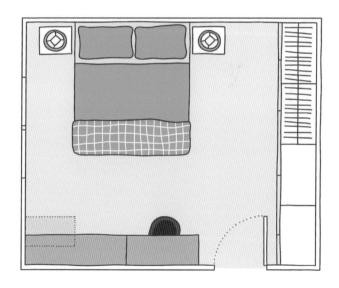

Where you position your double bed is personal taste, but can make a difference to how big the space appears.

Tips & tricks

NARROW, BUILT-IN FURNITURE

Built-in furniture is the key to success in a small-space bedroom. When installing your drawers and wardrobes, focus on building upwards not outwards to increase the amount of storage available. Long, slim pieces will keep your floor space clear. You should also consider under-bed storage: pick a bed base with built-in drawers, or a mattress that lifts up to reveal integrated storage space.

USE ALL AVAILABLE SURFACE SPACE

Small bedrooms often lack surface space; these spots are vital for adding personality in the form of plants, vases, photo frames, trinkets and all those other personal touches that make a house a home. Make use of windowsills and think about adding radiator covers or wall-hung shelves to create surface space where there isn't any.

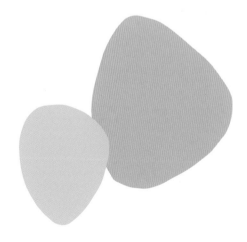

DITCH THE NIGHTSTAND!

When it comes to choosing between the largest mattress you can squeeze into your bedroom or having bedside tables, I would ALWAYS side with the bed. After all, you spend almost half your life there!

   If your bedroom is too narrow for bedside storage, there are plenty of alternative options. Choose wall lights or down lighting that can sit above your headboard. Look out for petite, wall-mounted bedside drawers, or if you have the opportunity, consider building a niche into your wall.

A BOLD BED

If your bedroom is teeny tiny, then giving your bed some serious wow factor is the way to go. A bold bed as the only thing in a cozy room will have serious impact. Choose colourful bedding, fabric headboards, patterns, prints and unexpected colour combinations.

The open-plan room

Open-plan floor plans, also called 'open concept', have been growing in popularity over the last decade, and whether designing a dinky studio or a generous barn conversion, multi-concept, open-plan design is as powerful as it is challenging to achieve.

Open-concept design can be defined as any floor plan that combines two or more rooms that are traditionally divided with a floor-to-ceiling wall or door. For example, the ever-popular kitchen-dining-living-room combination, where there are no dividing walls between any of the spaces.

How you go about designing yours will depend a lot on the shape and size of the space you are working with, and what architectural features already exist in the space.

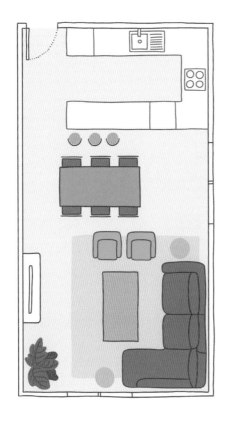

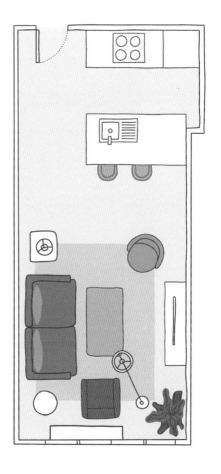

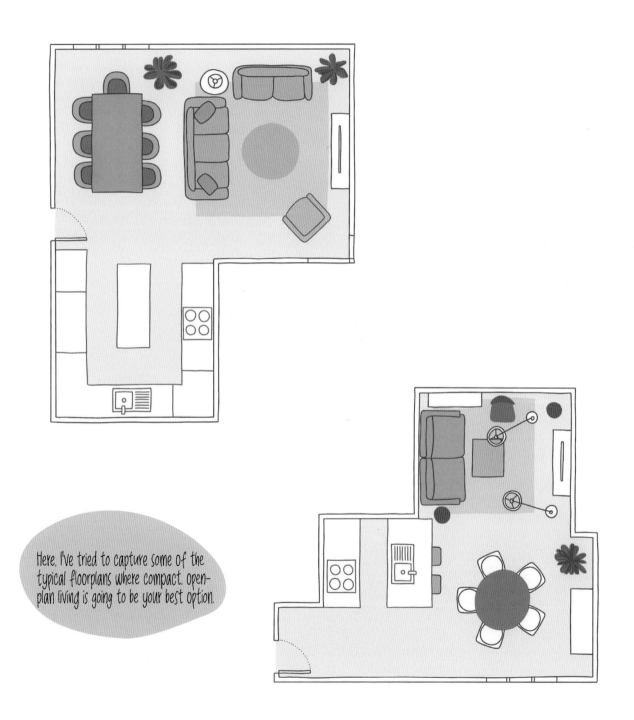

Here, I've tried to capture some of the typical floorplans where compact, open-plan living is going to be your best option.

PART THREE: THE BONUS ROUND – SMALL-SPACE LAYOUTS

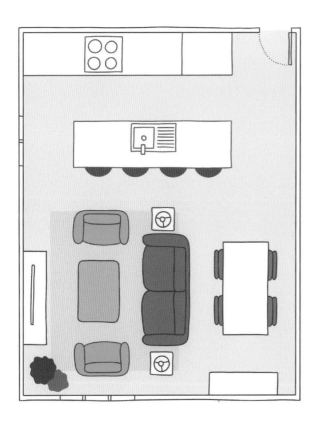

These floorplans show a kitchen with an island and a more traditional layout.

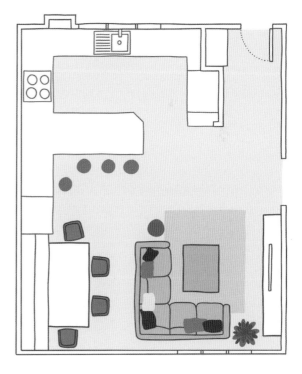

Tips & tricks

USE RUGS TO CREATE ZONES

Rugs are one of the quickest and most effective ways to create zones in open-concept living, without the need for any costly building work or bespoke furniture. An oversized rug visually defines and delineates areas in an open space. In small-space, open-concept design, it's highly likely you will only have space for one fabulous rug (in larger open-plan spaces, multiple, different-but-linked rugs are used to achieve the same thing). If this is the case, you should consider using an area rug in either the living or the dining zone.

You want the rug to anchor your space. The rug almost becomes a room in its own right, an island slightly separated from the dining or kitchen areas in the same space. In smaller spaces, ensure all your furniture is positioned entirely on the rug. If you are using a rug to zone your living space and have a little more room to play with, then as a minimum, you will want the front two feet of your seating fully on the rug.

USE COLOUR TO DISTINGUISH BETWEEN THE ZONES

Sheila Shed is a great example of how colour can be used to create distinguishable but linked zones. Come up with a colour palette in your planning phase, picking multiple, contrasting but complementary shades. Allocate these shades to different zones in your space.

COHESION, COHESION, COHESION

The key to successful open-concept design is being able to distinguish between the zones, while keeping the space connected, cohesive and whole. There are many subtle ways to achieve this, but ultimately, what you are trying to do is create a common 'thread' that pulls all the spaces together. Consider using some or all of the techniques listed over the page to achieve cohesion.

COLOURS

Be it in a cushion, a plant pot, a rug, wallpaper or paint, the repetition of a single colour throughout your open-plan space is a super simple and highly effective way to pull it together. By bringing colour from one space to another, but allowing for differentiation in each, the spaces are linked together but don't exactly match (retaining that distinction between uses). In Shelia Shed I placed at least one sage green plant pot in each zone of the studio; this pulled all the zones together, creating cohesion via a repeated, familiar colour highlight.

SHAPES

The repetition of shape and form is something that professional designers do often, but the lines can be so subtle that you don't even realize what's responsible for the success of the space – keep a beady eye on those soft curves and hard angles. Your furniture, artwork, lighting and accessories should all sit well together, and similarity in shape will help you achieve this. If you have an abstract painting in one space, take inspiration from its shapes in other areas. Don't suddenly switch to soft florals for example; this will lead to a mismatch.

LIGHTING

Similar or repeated lighting across zones will create a sense of familiarity and togetherness. Consider buying lights from the same family; they may differ in size, colour or finish, but if they are the same shape and style, they will contribute to that all-important thread between your spaces.

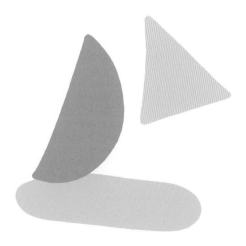

PART THREE: THE BONUS ROUND – SMALL-SPACE LAYOUTS

FLOORING

Use the same flooring throughout your small, open-plan space. While larger open-plan spaces lend themselves to multiple floor finishes and interesting transitions, our smaller abodes will benefit more from consistency. The use of one floor type throughout greatly increases the sense of space, avoiding visual interruptions created by door bars, floor strips and changes in the floor surface.

PARTITION WALLS

One vast open space that is devoid of structure can be especially hard to design and get right, even on a small scale. Partition walls can help here, physically separating one zone from another. Whether a solid wall, a bookshelf, a glass wall or a room divider, partition walls are a great tool for making open-concept living work for you.

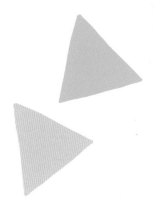

Small But Mighty Endings

Interior design has the power to profoundly impact our lives.

These are BIG words! but the truth is this, the way we design our homes has been proven to influence our behaviour, our mood and our overall well-being. I see it, I feel it, I believe it.

However, when dealing with small spaces, we tend to be thrown into sheer utter panic 'But where will everything go? It's just not going to work! If only I had more room!' The power of interior design, therefore, becomes even more significant when we are tackling modest spaces.

While many people find themselves living in small spaces out of necessity, an increasing number are actively choosing to embrace a simpler, smaller lifestyle. Smaller homes are eco-friendly, and homeowners can enjoy benefits such as reduced cleaning time, lower running expenses and diminished stress from managing mortgages and bills. Many small homeowners discover they have more time for hobbies and adventures as a result. Having experienced this personally, I can attest to this truth.

In writing *Small Space Big Living*, my first book, my goal was to create a practical and approachable step-by-step guide to small space interior design. The idea that this unpretentious and honest guide – born from lived experience – might give everyday people with modest homes and modest budgets, the confidence to take on design projects, fills me with happiness and that warm fuzzy glow that can't be bought – so thank you.

As this book concludes so too does our Shelia Shed journey. When we started our small-space adventure, we ambitiously believed that we might be living small for 12–18 months. In the end, this family of four lived in our bijoux abode for 29 months.

Was it easy? Hell no! Was it perfect? Is anything?! But... hand on heart, it was the small-space interior design techniques used in the creation of Sheila Shed, and shared with you in this book, that allowed us to not only survive but thrive!

We created a pint-sized home, full of personality, that is unbelievably functional, and we did this with the careful and considered use of:

- Multifunctionality
- Colour
- Zoning
- Bespoke Furniture
- Natural Light
- Symmetry and Asymmetry
- Biophilic Design
- Strategic Styling
- Clever Layout

By using the techniques, tips and tricks I've shared, you too can reach the heady heights of a home that is as functional as it is beautiful, regardless of its size or shape.

I believe that no matter your space or your budget, you can create magazine-worthy interiors without professional assistance. Achieving this level of excellence, however, requires a solid understanding of the techniques that will get you there, along with some good old-fashioned graft. Luckily, this book has you covered when it comes to the techniques!

My dream is that this book inspires others to make bolder, braver and better-informed Interior Design decisions, so seeing your *Small Space Big Living* inspired projects would quite literally be a dream come true. Please find me on Instagram @threeboysandapinkbath and share your projects, you can also follow along with the next installment of, our never-ending home renovation story.

Thank you for buying and reading this book, it means the world.
And remember,
Big things come in small packages and if I can do it, so can you!

Love Sofie, and of course, Sheila x

Resources

Seek out local trustworthy suppliers if you can. Here are some suggestions for suppliers to get you started.

B&Q
diy.com

Check A Trade
checkatrade.com

Elle Décor
elledecor.com

Farrow & Ball
farrow-ball.com

Frank Lloyd Wright
franklloydwright.org

Ikea
ikea.com

Livingetc
livingetc.com

MyBuilder
mybuilder.com

Pinterest
uk.pinterest.com

SmartDraw
smartdraw.com

***Sunday Times* Home supplement**
thetimes.com/life-style/property-home

About the author

Sofie Hepworth is an award-winning, colour-loving, digital content creator, interior stylist and product designer. She shares her incredible renovation projects on her colourful Instagram page @threeboysandapinkbath which has over 100K followers.

Sofie has been a professional content creator for more than four years, collaborating with hundreds of leading home and family lifestyle brands during that time, including, B&Q, American Express, Sofa.com, Vario by Velux, John Lewis, Made.com, Marks & Spencer, eBay and West Elm and she has also featured in *The Sunday Times Home* supplement, *House Beautiful*, *Ideal Home*, *Metro*, *Elle Décor* and *Living Etc.*

Stylist magazine named her 'The UK's most influential creator for colour'.

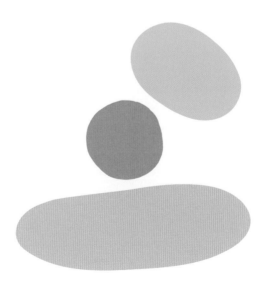

Index

INDEX

Acknowledgements

I'm a greater believer in luck, and I find the harder I work, the more I have of it. — My Dad, via Thomas Jefferson

The opportunity to write this book seemingly landed on my lap when a feature in The Sunday Times home supplement led to numerous publishers reaching out, all with the belief that Sheila Shed was a book and mine was a voice that people wanted to hear.

Writing the acknowledgments for this, my very first book, is a surreal experience but clichéd as it may sound, there are so many people without whom this book would not exist.

To my husband, Rob: my saviour, my best friend, and the biggest cheerleader I could ever wish for. You have taught me the meaning of unconditional love, and seeing myself through your eyes has enabled me to accomplish things I never thought possible. Your patience and understanding through countless renovations, business ideas and risky undertakings know no bounds. Writing a book while raising two young children, working full-time, running small businesses and building our family home is no small feat. Without your unwavering support, love and belief in me, I would not have achieved any of it. I would not eat, sleep or breathe without you. Thank you from the bottom of my heart.

To my stylish Mum, from whom I inherited any talent I may possess: your contributions have been invaluable. Thank you for all the years of making sandwiches on your hands during countless dusty renovations, for the endless house moves, the big clean-ups, the shopping trips, the shelf styling, the window cleaning, the childcare, the holidays, and your honest (not always asked for, LOL) opinions. I've never known a Mum or Nanna who gives more than you.

To my Dad, the wise owl who instilled in me a strong work ethic, determination and a desire to succeed: your words may be few, but they are always powerful. I admire you more than you will ever know.

To my followers on social media: without your years of encouragement and applause for all that I do, without you, I might never have overcome my imposter syndrome (which I'm still working on), I might never have considered myself a designer, and I might never have learned to be unapologetically me. While social media sometimes gets a bad reputation,

it has opened up opportunities that, the me of ten years ago, could only have dreamed up, and that is because of you, my community.

To my agents at the Soho Agency and my publisher: thank you for taking a chance on me and for your endless patience and guidance.

To Danny, my photographer, who has captured the last eight years of my life, through a camera lens. What a ride it's been, I can't wait for the next chapter.

And finally, a huge thank you to my beautiful boys, Teddy and Reggie, for whom I work so hard. In your short lives, you have already experienced countless of Mummy's crazy ideas, including sharing our tiny home while we build a dream together. I hope you look back on this time as a grand adventure. I hope I make you proud.

Quarto

First published in 2025 by Frances Lincoln
an imprint of The Quarto Group.
One Triptych Place,
London,
SE1 9SH
United Kingdom
T (0)20 7700 9000
www.Quarto.com

EEA Representation, WTS Tax d.o.o., Žanova ulica 3, 4000 Kranj, Slovenia

A catalogue record for this book is available from the British Library.

ISBN 978 0 7112 9046 4
Ebook ISBN 978 0 7112 9047 1

10 9 8 7 6 5 4 3 2 1

Photographer: Daniele Boggi
Floorplans and Illustrations: Joanna Rosado Illustration

Publisher: Philip Cooper
Art Director: Paileen Currie
Designer: Rachel Cross
Senior Production Controller: Rohana Yusof

Printed in China